JOSEPH COVINO JR

BERKELEY *BASHED:* VICTIM'S GUIDE TO THE BACKWARD, BARBARIC, BUTT-*UGLY* BOG

EPIC PRESS

Published by:
Epic Press
PO Box 30108
Walnut Creek, CA 94598
First *Epic Press* Edition published 2005

This book was printed proudly using politically incorrect ink and paper!

PROUDLY *dedicated*
to
the students
of
STANFORD
UNIVERSITY,
for making the smart-est, wisest and best choice of schools that Cal students might've and would've made—could they only have gotten in!

DUTIFUL DISCLAIMER

Your existence(sub-sistence or stagnation)and experience in the backward, barbaric, butt-UGLY *Bog of Berkeley* may differ and vary somewhat from that most undeniably and indisputably experienced(suffered and endured)firsthand by the writer of this book. In that extraordinary event, then, you've been most heavenly, miraculously and supernaturally BLESSED!

In no way as well—THANKFULLY— am I(the Berkeley BASHER!)at all even remotely related to that pretentious pretender of a "writer," *Michael Covino: that royally FRUSTRATED movie "critic" who used to "write" for the East Bay Excess, habitually giving away whole film plots and endings and bitterly bad-mouthing and panning the most richly successful BLOCK-BUSTER movie-makers(pompously telling THEM where THEY go WRONG and how HE thinks THEY should make THEIR movies!!!)!*
Only somebody enjoying a fully FAILED screen-writing career of his own could afford to be so outrageously RIDICULOUS!!!

CONTENTS

*"**FUCK** that Berkeley Bashed book!"*— Berkeley's *"Hate"* Man("falsely quoted")

OPENING PRAYER

*"An **ETERNITY** I've been imprisoned in this place!"*—evil, tear-ful extraterrestrial alien in *Star Trek V: The Final Frontier*

That forlorn alien's tragic sentiments echo exactly my own about the time stolen out of my own life that I've been condemned, sentenced and doomed to suffer as personal punishment, lying by force under compulsion and financial necessity alone, to waste and while away in the backward, barbaric, butt-UGLY Bog of Berkeley.

So I pray devoutly and fervently to God the Almighty and Heavenly Father, the First Cause and Creator of all Things: that He may have mercy on my eternal soul and, by my little book, count my time horrendously consumed by the Bog toward cutting drastically short my time sentenced to be spent in
PURGATORY!

For time frittered away in the Bog is, after all, tantamount to time frittered away in
HELL!!!

JOSEPH COVINO JR

FREE SPEECH CODES THIS BOOK DEVOTEDLY ADHERES TO AND ABIDES BY:

"I disapprove of what you say, but I will defend to the death your right to say it."—Friends of Voltaire, 1906

"Congress shall make no law respecting an establishment of religion, or prohibiting the free exercise thereof; or abridging the freedom of speech, or the press; or the right of the people peaceably to assemble, and to petition the government for a redress of grievances."—First Amendment to the United States Constitution

JOSEPH COVINO JR

ODE TO BERKELEY: CESSPOOL OF THE COSMOS

How do I love thee—Berserkeley? Let me count the ways.
I love thee to the length and breadth of your starkly barren and desolate wasteland.
My legs may stride, when standing up to my ankles in litter and trash, wading and rummaging my way blindly, through your enchanting wonderland of garbage and graffiti.
To the far reaches of un-reality and recycled radiance.
I love thee to the uttermost limits of everyone's
Coldest and most perverse and perverted longing, for chronic cloudiness and gloom.
I love thee grudgingly, as frustrated, up-tight pretentious progressives fight for fanatical extremist Self-Right:
I love thee facetiously, as they wallow in their self-indulgent Hollowness and Hypocrisy.
I love thee with a love I'm for sure to lose—the longer I'm forced to while and waste away in your vile, violent and vulgar sewer:
With my long-lost friends and loves—I love thee with my most retching gag and gasp.
Regrets, relics and refuse of all my life—and, God willing, I will surely love thee best once I'm dead and gone to decay, far, far away, from your infernal, paranoiac PIT!

JOSEPH COVINO JR

PROFILE OF THE PC STALKER

My name's JERK the Ripper. I'm a serial killer and mass murderer—a rapist of the mind. And I cordially invite you to take an intimate and introspective look into my own self-stroked ego and self-flattered mind.

I'm of very unsound mind, for you see, I suffer a supreme superiority complex.

I'm a proud, puerile posturer—pompous and pretentious—though I'm profoundly confused about what I have to be so proud of.

I follow the human herd: I cherish no beliefs or opinions of my own; I carry no conscientious convictions of my own; I'm content—that is, smugly complacent—in taking cowardly refuge in mob mentality.

And I'm much too intelligent and intellectual, much too educated and enlightened, much too scholarly and sophisticated, much too cultured and cosmopolitan, much too matchless and modern to hold a belief in anything higher or greater than myself—much less, dare I mention(Heaven forbid!)the unmentionable: God! Or religion! Or faith! I'm so stupidly SUPERIOR.

Pseudo-Progressive Piety is the irrational rationalism—that is, rationalization—that gives me my right to relentlessly pillage and plunder human minds other than my own.

Compulsion is my sacred(and sacrosanct)cult and creed. If you don't want to know about my culture, my ethnicity, my race, my sex—freely, willingly, for learning's sake—then I'll MAKE you learn. I'll FORCE myself on you until you completely submit and pretend that I engage and engross you(if not gross you out!), interest and intrigue you. My unfettered right to rape your unsuspecting mind is utterly absolute. I'm so stupidly SUPERIOR.

I'm so sensitive too—more about myself and my own extremist, fanatical fixations and frustrations than anything or anyone else. I'm so oppressed, repressed and suppressed, though I'm supremely uncertain of who's doing so much wrong and injustice to me. I'm such a whining VICTIM, I can't positively identify my victimizers, so I must in turn victimize, whoever and wherever I can.

I preach, sermonize and moralize—and you HAVE to listen and learn your lessons well, or else I'll FORCE you. Raping minds is my absolute right. I'm so stupidly SUPERIOR.

And you'd better be real careful of what you say and how you speak to me: you just might unwittingly offend my most simplistic sensitivity—the misguided and misinformed notion that my ethnicity and race make up my entire culture.

You're allowed neither free thought nor speech, neither personal choice nor opinion. I pretentiously pretend that I'm tolerant. But

*I tolerate no one unless they mindlessly con-
form to what I think and believe. I'm tolerant
so long as you don't inconvenience or otherwise offend me. Forced brainwashing and indoctrination—thought control—make up my
perfect practice of tolerance. That's what I
call FREE-THINKING!*

*Yes, I'm so sanctimonious and self-righ-
teous. Hypocrisy is my deepest, darkest, most
dogmatic doctrine. My favorite style is to shout
down and stifle anyone who fails to fall in with
it. I'm surly, snarling and sarcastic. I've got
an attitude. I'm childishly contrary and con-
frontational. I'm so stupidly SUPERIOR.*

*My ethnicity, my race, my sex—I'm so differ-
ent, so self-conscious, so wishfully SPECIAL,
so over-OBSESSED with myself. I'm a self-interested, self-indulgent GROUPIE of gender
and color. My cultural identity IS my gender
and color—not my common HUMANITY. I'm
so self-indignant and doctrinaire. I'm so stupidly SUPERIOR.*

*Hate, hostility and ritualized resentment
are my sole driving forces. I have ever so
many chips on my shoulders, ever so many
hang-ups, I'm weighed down to the point of
complete collapse. And I'll coerce and intimidate you with all of them until you chime in:
I'm so used, abused and misused. I harbor so
many grudges, I have so many axes to grind,
that if you refuse to chime in: I just may bury
one of them in your brain! Tolerance means
tyranny, and I'll tyrannize YOU until you completely capitulate and conform.*

Nothing and no one are sacred of course—

least of all past tradition. I'm so intellectually IMPOTENT that I must constantly criticize instead of create, crush instead of construct. And I'll crush you if you mess with my criminally crippled mind. I'll burden you with my own crushing guilt!

More, I'm a subjugating subversive. I subject everyone to myself because everyone else OWES me—deference because I'm different, special treatment because I'm oh-SO special. I'm justly entitled and liberated at everyone else's expense—and hand-outs. After all, the whole wide world revolves around none but me.

I'm so intellectually STERILE that I simply must stalk and kill, resorting and reverting to the extreme narrowness of my own extremely closed mind—not to mention the redundance of my harping harangue.

Yes, I'm JERK the Ripper—the serial stalker and killer of the truly free, free-thinking mind.

I'm POLITICALLY CORRECT and I'm coming to condemn, castigate—and correct!—you!

PROLOGUE: FEELING FREE TO *BASH* BERKELEY

"Berkeley, with its unique combination of brains, beauty, and bohemia, is like no other city in the United States."—City•*Stupid*: Berkeley Oakland

JOSEPH COVINO JR

Greetings and salutations! I'm the Berkeley **BASHER!** And yes indeed this book's all about bashing, battering and breaking down the blighted Bastion of outright Hypocrisy and Pretention that *IS* the backward, barbaric and butt-**UGLY** Bog of Berkeley! And so it's also a book about and *for* true **FREE SPEECH**—preserving it, protecting it, defending it!

It's also a book beating most adamantly against what I call the witlessly and unthinkingly **PASSIVE, PUPPET-ICALLY CORRECT** movement—overobsessed and preoccupied as it is with the most trifling and trivial matters of utter indifference(like: where does the Bog really rank on that illusory scale of "diversity?" Or which toilet on Cal campus sports the most poetic graffiti?)rather than matters of vital importance or crucial consequence.

And the movement's up-tight pretentious progressives, as I call them, remain fanatically obsessed with taking extremely relentless but patently unrealistic pains to avoid *offending* the trite and tired sensibilities—especially the most *semantic* ones—of just about anyone and everyone—especially if they happen to be among those most exclusive and special "people of color!" In the very same hypocritical, intolerant and pretentious breath, though, they'll just as stubbornly(or stupidly)self-indulge, coddle and cater with self-important, self-indignant and self-righteous fury to all their endlessly rabid and raging **RESENTMENTS**: so ponderous and heavy are all the ever so many semantic shoulder-chips weighing these pedantic pretenders down, their brains as well as their knees will be buckling on the brink of collapse until the crack of doom!

Well, Punks—listen up, check this out and get a clue once and for all time: our dearly precious and sacred

First Amendment guarantees *NO ONE* the freedom *FROM* giving or taking *OFFENSE!* Got that? Good!

Berkeley is a "city," so-called, of countless and continuous come-ons(you can't walk one frickin' block anyplace in the entire backward, barbaric, butt-*UGLY* Bog without getting accosted by somebody for something!)and so it's also a "city," so-called, of persistent and perennial **PARANOIA**(just watch the fearfully shifty eyes of cringing and cowering passerby as they skulk and slink past you on those celestial "city" streets—especially 'fraidy cat little girls!)! So thank *GOD!*—it's all to the good that the Bog is like no other cesspool in the cosmos much less the United States!

Flying in the stark, staring face of all truth and reality, though, the Bog's most pretentious pretenders persist with making the insidiously false claim that they live in some whimsically "progressive" and politically correct never-never land. Well, that's the glorified, made-up, make-believe and **MYTHOLOGICAL** Chamber-of-Commerce side of the Bog. This book presents, finally, that other, unadulterated, factual, real and **TRUE** side of the Bog!

Lots of bitter Bog-Bugs, as I call them, aren't going to like that, naturally—and that's just too frickin' bad about them! And instead of rebutting with logical, rational or even reasoned discussion or debate they'll readily and predictably prove my point by resorting and reverting with reflex action to back-biting and name-calling, trying ineffectually to belittle and run me down personally with virulent vulgarity and infantile invective—and I could care *LESS!* It's to be prophetically expected, though, since bitter Bog-Bugs simply cannot bear or stand even the slightest **SEMBLANCE** of any sort of criticism or fault-finding whatever! Their baseless Bog is, after all, supposed to be the perfect paragon of paradise the world over! Yeah, right.

Those bitter Bog-Bugs suffering the most deathly and deep-seated **FEAR** of any sort of effective rebuttal to the profound profusion of bombastic platitudes, propaganda and outright **BULL** about the Bog they churn out so redundantly and relentlessly to captive reading audiences, day after insufferable day, are of course the ego-endangered "editors," so-called, of the Bog's most incredibly illegitimate, ad-glutted litter-box-liner rags: the *Berkeley Daily Planet*(the supreme puffery paper that would be more appropriately titled the *Bizarro World Gazette!*), the *Berkeley Voice*(the unmuted mouthpiece for the Bog Establishment!), the *Daily Cal*(the most colossal student contribution to the recycled paper industry under the sun!), the *East Bay Express*(or *Excess*—the neverending editorial–posing–as–a–sham–of–a–feature–article that specializes in photographing and pretentiously posing the outright butt-*UGLIEST* people it can find to glare and glower into the camera!)and, not to mention, the *Monthly*(Emeryville's encyclopedic-sized paid commercial advertisement!)!

The *East Bay Excess* in particular, fantasizes the *Insider's* guide, "...runs thoughtful essays...and some of it is written with an attitude that matches Berkeley's." Yep, brain-dead editorials posing as news features epitomizing the Bog's rampant pedantic pretension!

They specialize similarly in censoring any written word freely expressing, exposing and showing up the free-speech fallacy about the Bog—simply because it effectively differs, disagrees with and disposes of their passively, puppet-ically correct agenda! They most conveniently and expediently forget that most noble notion of disapproving of, disputing and even denouncing something somebody said or wrote but defending to the death their perfectly legitimate and unassailable right to say or write it!

Well, dear readers, all that's about to change—drastically and **RADICALLY** for the better!—with just about the stiffest and severest **SHOT** of honest, straightforward and outspoken **TRUTH**(set down in this book!)that bitter Bog-Bugs will likely now or ever see or take—*long* time in coming, *LONG* time overdue! Here they're about to learn that most invaluable lesson: the indelible and inalienable right of **FREE SPEECH** holds good and true for even the passive, puppet-ically correct '90s and beyond! Here the unfettered, untrammeled and unenthralled **TRUTH** will be neither stifled nor suppressed! Here the inescapable and unstoppable **TRUTH** will most inescapably and unstoppably *SET YOU FREE!*

This is incisive, intense and *SERIOUS SATIRE!* So if you can't take it, bitter Bog-Bug **BABIES**, then take the very same sassy advice you so smugly lecture, preach and sermonize to everyone else: *DON'T FRICKIN' READ IT!*

For roughly two decades you've been right up in my face—rabidly carping at, harping on and haranguing me and everybody else! I'm fed up! I've had enough! I'm hopping mad as hell and I'm not going to take it anymore! Now it's *MY TURN!* Now it's *PAYBACK TIME!*

I *AM* the Berkeley **BASHER!** And I'm coming to **BASH** *YOU!!!*

PREFACE:
BOGUS
BERKELEY

"Berkeley looms large in the national psyche, and yet it's hard to fit a face to the name—like any other hip and happening cosmopolitan paradise, Berkeley has many faces."—Guide To The "Good Life" in Berkeley

JOSEPH COVINO JR

Self-conscious, self-deceiving, self-deluding, self-glorifying, self-important *in the extreme* the backward, barbaric, butt-***UGLY*** Bog of Berkeley would like to think—*think*, I say—that no matter how ridiculously absurd and incredibly far-fetched the notion is: miraculously, improbably and hopelessly contrary to all reasonable, rational expectation Berkeley somehow still shines forth and counts for something meaningful, momentous or memorable which is, in turn, indelibly impressed onto our national consciousness! All put together such arrogrant presumption, pomposity and pretension add up to the sum total of Berkeley's most high-flown, bombastic, grandiose and vainglorious **WISHFUL THINKING!!!** And only the Bog could pile up its own dungheap to a peak and pinnacle of such mountainous proportions!

For decades now the Bog has struggled fruitlessly to immortalize itself in our national consciousness by sailing so falsely on the lofty laurels of that made-up, make-believe reputation of that long-gone, long-lost Aquarian age and '60s generation—like some aging hipster still straining today to milk past glory by trading on outmoded hit parades! And tragically the so-called Spirit of the Sixties has long since died its notably ignoble death! Tragically, I say, since the original '60s spirit was at least creative and inventive. Put in its place at present is of course the extravagantly senseless, silly, stupid and passively, pre-programmed **PUPPET-ICALLY CORRECT MOVEMENT**—witless and un-thinking *in the extreme!*

Supposedly the backward, barbaric, butt-UGLY Bog of Berkeley is possessed of ever so many facets and aspects when the plain, unvarnished truth is—it has only one, single, solitary face: *shallow superficiality!* And for many the cold, sober truth will be too hard to take.

But that's just too bad. So before reading any further be fully forewarned: this book won't shirk or shy away from exposing the truth about the Bog—once and for all time—solely to avoid offending the sappy sensibilities of the ever so easily offended. So before we even start getting to it poor, bitter Bog-Bug babies: ***GET OVER IT!!!***

Because: even though the Bog ferociously makes believe and pretends—with all the fanatical fervor of some rabid revolutionary—that somehow it still embodies the imaginary progressive paradise of multi-cultural tolerance and diversity, so on and so forth, ad nauseam, ad infinitum, only one popular buzzword can totally and truthfully sum up the Bog's perpetual and imperishable phoniness: ***BOGUS!!!***

FOREWORD:

LAND

OF THE

LIVING

DEAD

"But then, Berkeley isn't any other community."—Insider's Guide: Berkeley And The East Bay

JOSEPH COVINO JR

T his book directly rebuts and talks straight back to a supremely pretentious, propagandizing, commercial advertisement-glutted guidebook(published in 1994 by "Good Life Publications"—in *Stanford* no less!—re-published in 2003 in Santa Clara)promoting by its fabricated title the so-called "good life in Berkeley."

Good life? What frickin' good life???!!!

If you are so cruelly cursed that you're forced to actually live in Berkeley for any interminable lapse of time, for whatever apology or excuse, and you are actually still breathing or even just barely able to draw breath, then you can count yourself mightily lucky indeed: for Berkeley as an infernal place of torment—a literal hell on earth—could very well be likened to a land of the living dead!

Berkeley's trapped, lifelong, eternally condemned inmates typically look more like walking dead zombies than healthy, hearty, thriving human beings. For the most part they look luridly, deathly pale, sickly, shattered, decrepit—and for very good reason: they mostly *are* simply by *being* in Berkeley. Only dull, lifeless oblivion shows through their deeply dazed but abysmally empty eyes.

At best "life" in Berkeley is idle and static subsistence. At worst it's utter, stupefying stagnation.

Good life in Berkeley???!!! If you do just happen to be actually alive and living in Berkeley then you truly are powerfully lucky simply to be alive: for the longer you perilously try your luck by forcing yourself to stay stuck and stranded there you're as good as dead already—or at least as good as bordering on the very brink of being quite thoroughly, quite soundly, stone cold dead!

Other guidebooks, so-called, equally eulogize the living dead of the Bog. The City•*Stupid* guide volunteers its tips, trivia and even its "top 10" lists. The *Insider's* Guide volunteers its "close-ups"(which this book correctly re-names *reality checks!*), "insider's" tips and even the occasional "caution"—which this book correctly re-names the *black flag warning!* And the "good life" guide volunteers its "favorites," "perfect one day trips" and "slices of life"—which this book correctly re-names *Rejects, Perfect Escapes* and *Bits of the Bog!*

"*The Insider's Guide to Berkeley and the East Bay* attempts to mirror the process of meeting someone and then becoming friends," fawns Bog booster, Carol Fowler, who quite revealingly lives not in the abominable Bog but rather in the more upscale, gentrified and yuppiefied suburban town of *Walnut Creek!*

Doubtless she with *truth* wouldn't wish the living dead of the Bog on her worst enemy much less any newfound friend!

Back in *2001* Cal's recycled student paper, the **Daily Cull**, blazoned one of its "orientation" inserts with that incredibly original banner headline: a *Berkeley odyssey*—alluding of course to that arduously plodding film of a similar name!

Odyssey misguidedly implies some marvelous and wondrous journey. **ORDEAL**—and its attendant trials, tribulations and **ADVERSITY**—is in reality what you'll more accurately experience in Berkeley. Other choice "alternative" glossology more precisely particularizes the Berkeley experience: *absurdity, buffoonery, idiocy, inanity, insanity, lunacy—**TRAVESTY!!!**(anything but* odyssey!)!

"This book is to help you enjoy the best of Berkeley...," puffs the "good life" guide.

THIS book, conversely, is to help you appreciate the unvarnished truth that the so-called "best" of the Bog is its utmost **WORST** and vice versa!

BITS OF THE BOG
BERKELEY'S *REAL* NAME

Reportedly, Berkeley got named after an aspiring but blundered Anglo-Irish pioneer cleric, George Berkeley, who never even found his way to America much less California, even after putting into verse that notorious poetic line, *"Westward the course of empire takes its way."* It would doubtless gall the Bog's fanatically rabid athiestic conclave to learn that its beloved "progressive" Nirvana was named after an early 18th-century British *Bishop* of Cloyne!

Well, following in George's royally frustrated footsteps to this very day Berkeley is and remains over-populated—polluted, really—by countless, untold hordes of ever proliferating wanna-bes and would-bes of every possible breed and brood imaginable—each and all rushing headlong on their own separate fast track to nowhere!

"Berkeley's international reputation as an intellectual mecca and a dynamic social center continues to make it a magnet for inventive people and new ideas."—official visitors guide

More in keeping with the critical tone of this treatise, then, we could more aptly and readily re-phrase George's lyrical line to read:

"Berkeleyward the inevitable, inexorable course of foul, fecal excrement works its heaving, expulsive way to the deepest, most abysmal bowels of our earth!"

The backward, barbaric, butt-**UGLY** Bog of Berkeley is, as a matter of true course, both the figurative and literal **CESSPOOL OF THE COSMOS!**

What the Bog's bestial "magnet" actually attracts are aspiring **GUTTER RATS!!!**

BERKELEY: THE BIRD'S EYE-DROPPING VIEW

As tourism and travel advertisement publicity will no doubt try to gull and beguile you to believe the backward, barbaric, butt-*UGLY* Bog of Berkeley holds out to potential visiting victims and prey the very dubious and tenuous prospect of a richly mixed variety of singular settings and surroundings to experience, explore and enjoy. Well, my dear gullible readers, don't be duped or otherwise roped in royally by such false, fraudulent and defecating propaganda. If you do let yourself be so fooled then you've already been made a royal ass of.

The pure and unadulterated truth is, the Bog can lay claim to only this twofold fame: *aggravation and abomination!*

So no matter where or when in the Bog you may go, or whatever you may set out to do, you can set your unsuspecting, unwitting heart on suffering and enduring those two things.

That you can take straight to the Bank of America!

CHAPTER ONE: ACCOSTING ARTISTRY IN THE BOG

Spare Change?

"Panhandling is not as prevalent as it used to be here...You're more likely to be asked to buy a newspaper than for a handout on Telegraph Avenue or Shattuck Avenue."—City•**Stupid** guide

*"The City•**Stupid** guide minces the truth: the so-called 'homeless newspaper'('Street Spirit')you'll get stuck for will set you back a buck or **two** in handouts!"*—the Berkeley **BASHER**

JOSEPH COVINO JR

A*ccosting* is the single most all-encompass- ing, all-inclusive concept that most accu- rately and completely defines, describes and characterizes the backward, barbaric, butt- **UGLY** Bog of Berkeley. *Accosting* is the concept that most vividly and graphically exemplifies and personi- fies the Bog. *Accosting* is the concept that most clearly, absolutely and positively epitomizes and sums up the sum total of the Bog. *Accosting* **IS** the Bog's most com- prehensive and exhaustive description, definition and summary—precise and perfect. *Accosting* makes up and equates totally to what the Bog is really all about.

Almost no one anywhere in the whole, wide, butt- **UGLY** world of the Bog shows any common courtesy, consideration or respect whatever for any other per- son's personal space and proximity let alone privacy. In a nutshell *accosting* is what the Bog boils down to: you can't go anywhere or do anything in any quarter of the Bog without being accosted by somebody or some thing—typically some breed of **BUG!** And the Berkeley **Bog-Bug** has only one real aim, ambition or aspiration in life as its sole reason or rationale for even existing much less for persisting in the Bog: to **BUG HELL**— meaning to bother, badger, pester, harass, molest, an- noy, aggravate, irritate, infuriate and exasperate—you and everybody else all over, all around and all across the entire length and breadth of the backward, barbar- ic, butt-**UGLY** Bog!

To be more specific let's now go into exact and ex- acting detail and spell out precisely what this means for you—the prospective prey and victim making the very misguided mistake of ever so stupidly blundering your way to the butt-**UGLY** Bog of Berkeley.

Here's just some of the countless ways you can count on getting *accosted*:

In sight of Sather Gate on Sproul Plaza on the University of California(variously also known as UC-Berkeley, Cal or just the university)campus ideology and idiocy go hand in hand!

Says the "good life" guide:

"Step onto famed **Sproul Plaza**, *site of the infamous free speech battles of the 60s and many more modern protests, and you'll instantly become a piece of urban theater. Street philosophers spout theories, street people sleep on benches, serious academic types mill about, and bands of tourists roam freely in search of the exotic. On Sproul, you can never be sure which person is the professor and which is the unemployed poet, but the guessing game is endlessly amusing."*

Says City•*Stupid:*

"...political activists of every bent still staff their tables and ask passerby to sign their petitions. Evangelists pray for the souls of the passing sinners. Cadres of musicians play night and day, including a constant contingent of drummers. The best time to catch the action is the middle of the day."

Says the *Insider's* Guide:

"This is the heart of the campus for students. It's where they mingle with each other, with street people, neighbors, and nursery school kids out for a stroll with their caregivers. It's a lively scene, especially at noon. Musicians perform, and political, religious and social activists set up tables and talk to(or harangue)the crowd."

Those are the putting–it–mildly understatements. Here's the real undisguised and undistorted lowdown:

•political fanatics of every conceivable faction—each and all as dogmatic, narrow-minded and intolerant as the other—will come at you with their handbills, leaflets, fliers and petitions—all the while spouting and spewing forth their pet philosophies.

•religious fanatics of every conceivable sect will relentlessly and tenaciously harangue you with their preachy sermons, striving zealously to consummate incorrigibly-inflicted conversions.

•social activists, so-called, demonstrators and protesters of every conceivable cause and complaint—going out and about among the crowded, great *unwashed*(often *literally!*)masses of common people only if and when doing so suits their expedient excuses—will rant, rave and raise their irate and indignant voices right in your face, bent on bullying and browbeating you into mental if not physical submission by challenging you to agree and favor them with your aid and support whether you want to give it or not! Or else!

•piss-poor "performers" of every conceivable amateurish assortment will batter you with their shamelessly exhibitionist but still downright inferior and mediocre displays and spectacles: so whether you're passing through Lower Sproul Plaza to get besieged and bombarded by the perennial clamor of the endless banging by supposed drummers and bongo-beaters, or passing by Hertz(as in *hertz your ears!*)and Morrison Halls(the supposed music buildings)to get beset and beleaguered by discordant ensemble groups, filling the air with their harshly unharmonious noise, you cannot escape getting your unwilling, unconsenting ears pierced by intrusive and disconcerting racket(note sympathetically that Cal music majors are reputedly compelled to master more musical theory than musical performance!).

Either that or some hooligan parading down the street carrying their ghetto-blasting "boom-box" loudly blares that hip-hop or rap racket—as if anybody willingly wanted to listen to that shit!

These wondrous campus environs literally dump

over onto Southside's Telegraph Avenue. Going south-ward from the chaotic clutter of the countless circu-lars posted and stapled onto poles and billboards all over Sproul Plaza and beyond you can plow your way through the windswept litter of the square to the even more esthetically pleasing experience of strolling an-kle-deep through trash on the smutty street.

Ah, yes, simply *enchanting!*

Strolling along Telegraph or almost any other avenue in the Bog truly is an absolute feast for all the senses: ugly and unsightly graffiti for the eyes; loud-mouthed yelling and shouting for the ears; the putrid stench of garbage, filth, fast-food slop, urine and motor vehicle exhaust fumes—all artfully blended together to put a positively nasty and gamy taste in your mouth! Yes, without doubt, the whole of the Bog is an unqualified, honest–to–goodness eyesore, sordid and squalid to a *T*—a perfect model of blight and squalor!

And on your merry way:

•panhandlers will aggressively bum(or abusively demand)your "spare change"(the more maddening among these being those very healthy and young run-away rebels—the grubby and grungy "gutter punks"—from rich suburban families mooching and sponging your money to fund and finance their adolescent angst and pathos by buying their pizza, beer and cigarettes!).

"Berkeley's live-and-let-live policies also draw foot-loose teenagers from across the country to Telegraph Avenue where they loll in pierced splendor," minces the City•*Stupid* guide. *Squalor*—not "splendor"—is the ac-tual reality.

•petitioners, mostly ineffectual, will solicit your sig-nature, typically asking first whether you're a registered California voter—to which I typically revel in replying, "Not no, but *hell* no! Now away with you, knave!"(more

amusing among these being those very passe social-
ists!).

•flunkies from smelly, run–of–the–mill restaurants
or retail outlets will aggressively hand out their circu-
lars and supposedly discounted food or sale coupons.

•hawkers(street "artisans" and "vendors" some presume to call them though I prefer referring to them by
their real name: *moneymongers!*)will peddle their persistently profuse piles of out–and–out, good–for–nothing ***JUNK(fraudulently misnamed "crafts")!!!***

Probably the Bog's paragon of its own blight and
squalor is the dingy and dumpy 2.8-acre plot of bleak
and barren university-owned land notoriously named
People's Park—the favorite stomping ground for the
drug-dealers, gutter punks, assorted violent hoodlums
and poor homeless folk squatting there—at least during the daytime before the Bog's imperious but utterly
useless penny-ante police run them out of *all* parks at
night(officially at 10pm).

Most amusing if not outright ridiculous was a
time past when the local bosses of the Bog actually
tried—laughably and ludicrously—to pitch and promote
People's Park to the outside world at large as a tourist attraction equal in appeal and popularity to *Disney
World!!!*

Ironically the Bog Landmarks Commission has designated that little tract of wasted wasteland—where one
person was *killed* during a May 1969 riot but where the
university would rather build a student dormitory if it
had its druthers—as a, get this!, "Monument to *Peace*."

Its original squatters in April 1969 dubbed it *Power
to the People Park*. But it's the university that held the
purse strings(and "power")when it purchased the park
for $1.3 million in June 1967 and still pulls the strings
to the present day.

"Do Something For Peace!" exhorts a sizable but scuzzy sign fronting an equally scuzzy property on Milvia Street in the northward Bog. Yeah, I'm always prompted to retort: like, erect yet *another* sizable but scuzzy sign! That's really *doing* something for peace!

One of *SF Chronicle* columnist Jon Carroll's "top 10 favorite things about the East Bay" is the so-called **Peace Grove** about three miles distant from *Inspiration Point* in *Tilden Park* "with its wooden plaques, many of them half *hidden*..." The Bog does well to hide, secrete and put out of sight as many of its token and pretentious *"peace"* gestures as it possibly can!

More weird and uncanny than any bizarre and outlandish vagrant("street person")are the local, more native Bog-Bug residents, especially those subsisting and stagnating in the south and west sides of that coastal plain area where slightly more than half the Bog is situated—euphemistically termed the *flats*. They mostly thrive on blight and wallow in squalor. For them the more blighted and squalid their neighborhoods the better!

•Why else would these madly bombastic, loud-mouthed crybabies constantly whine and complain each and every time some chain retail outlet tried setting up shop there, offering in bulk both economy-boosting jobs and high-quality, cut-rate goods—for fear that it just might actually spruce up and refurbish the place just a teeny-weeny little bit?

"Gentrification!" is their misguidedly rallying war cry! They stupidly—and wrongly—blame these beneficial chain stores for supposedly running smaller, independently-owned convenience stores(those selling the most extravagantly priced goods)out of business purely because the chains can afford to pay the exorbitant—extortionate, really—*rents* charged by *local*, greedy, landowning landlords!

Why else do the Bog's ever so caring and ecoloically and environmentally concerned citizens fall all over themselves so frantically to recycle their bottles, cans and newspapers(while begrudging and penalizing homeless people pushing shopping carts for laboring to eke out their most marginal living from recycling)but outright refuse to teach their own savage offspring, either through discipline or upbringing, some semblance of respect or consideration for the Bog's streets and property?

Why else does the Bog set loose to work on those selfsame filthy and smutty streets a literal legion of valiant and intrepid street-sweepers—at least during the summer months while visiting tourists are milling around the Bog—but turn a blind and indifferent eye to the barbaric brats who litter and graffiti the whole Bog right and left?

Why else does the Bog go out of its way to cite and fine so-called scavenging "poachers"(who would likely do a better and cheaper job of recycling than costly "city contractors")instead of wading first into the dumpheap, digging in and recycling the ankle-deep garbage and trash already littering the Bog's smutty streets where at night droves of ravenous rats run rampant?(Just hang out on the corners of Milvia and Addison or Center streets after dark to catch the scurrying nocturnal rodent activity!—an exhilarating Bog pastime!).

Why else then does the Bog fail time and time again to cite and fine those ever so many puerile punks(typically black)for dumping ever so freely and indiscriminately their fast food cellophane wrappers and plastic cups of ice and straws all over the frickin' place?

"Few urban areas are greener than Berkeley...," stupidly proclaims the City•*Stupid* guide. "People get passionate about the environment here."

To come to grips with the massive rubbish heap making up the Bog the Bog bosses—"As befitting one of America's recycling capitals"—need first to *GET A(**BIG**)GRIP* and get "passionate" about recycling all the filth, garbage, litter and trash permeating its not–so–"green" smutty streets!

Finally, forget worrying about muggers and robbers accosting you in the Bog though they do pose a notable threat to the Bog's public.

Posing the most chronic and habitual public menace to you while subsisting or stagnating in the Bog will be the rowdy, rude and unruly teenagers running rampant, roughshod and wild all over the frickin' Bog! Ill-bred and ill-mannered to a punk these obnoxious, foul-mouthed and vulgar hooligans and hoodlums will do their barbaric best to bully, curse, challenge, provoke, taunt and even violently attack you on the Bog's mostly lawless streets!

Having learned from neither parents nor teachers any respect or consideration for anyone or anything these savage, uncivilized, uncouth and unkempt punks will sneer, stare and swear at you as you pass by on the smutty streets of the Bog. Or they'll deliberately bump into you or will purposely spit onto your forward-stepping footpath just to start something—preferably a street fight or brawl!

They heartily believe that no laws or rules of civilized conduct or behavior apply to them in the least—and that even in heavy street traffic it's actually their civil right(especially if they're black)to saunter along crosswalks against red traffic lights or else to bang violently on the hoods or trunks of idling cars stopped at those red lights! Either that or they'll plod along the sidewalks in unruly mobs, trudging abreast of each other like doddering and decrepit old fogeys but taking up the entire frickin' sidewalk like it's their frickin' civil right to deliberately and purposely block the way so that other more naturally-paced pedestrians have no space to pass—instead of having the simple decency and courtesy to politely move their dragging asses to one side so that other people can share the sidewalk and pass them by!

And the Bog's imperious but utterly useless penny ante police will remain in hiding throughout and will be nowhere to be seen or found for help once the pugnacious punks do strike! So learn how to fight back and hold your own since you'll be strictly alone and on your own!

Berkeley High School, the *Insider's* guide stupidly apologizes, "sends kids to Harvard nearly every year, but still it has problems." Yeah, it has its "problems" all right: it's so barbaric and uncivilized it can barely keep a permanent principal in office and during its daily lunch periods it duly dispatches what the City•*Stupid* guide calls its "future Ivy League graduates" out to both *brawl and shop-lift* all around all over the frickin' Bog! Most Bog businesses post signs at their entrances typically limiting and restricting admittance of students to two at a time to curtail getting taken to the cleaners and getting their stock snitched!

You'll typically encounter and confront the Bog's most idle and lumpish teenaged punks loitering and hanging around the **BART**(*Bay Area Rapid Transit*)station situated at what is euphemistically called "downtown" Berkeley—one of the grossest and most grotesque parts of the Bog, harshly and heavily oppressive in its hopelessly desolate and desperate depression. Its smudged streets are so blackened with smut that even the Bog's most daring and determined street-sweepers can't *steam*-blast and scour them clean!

DOWNTOWN is such a silly, stupid **MISNO-MER!** Berkeley is neither a city nor a town nor even a burg—it's a frickin' **BOG**, pure and simple, and a backward, barbaric, butt-**UGLY** one at that!!!

Scattered all around the Bog are asinine prohibition signs stupidly proclaiming: *NUCLEAR-FREE ZONES*.

Pretty preposterous—not to mention laughable—once you consider that the Bog partly spawned the Atomic Age(much like local sacred cow, *Peet's Coffee*, partly spawned the *Starbucks* chain!): physicists Ernest Lawrence and Robert Oppenheimer pre-fabricated the world's deadliest and most murderous "weapons of mass destruction" exploiting the campus cyclotron and the nation's first radiation lab. Indeed, UC Berkeley "scientists" discovered ten of the elements on the periodic table, including *Berkelium, Californium*...and ***Plutonium!***

"Just gawking at the wild denizens of Telegraph Avenue can be eye-popping fun for kids," stupidly proclaims the City•*Stupid* guide, "but Berkeley and Oakland have considerably more to offer than a *freak* show."

Not much more! What the *"People's Republic of Berkeley"* really and truly needs, quite apart from *"Nuclear-Free Zones and Smoke-Free Zones,"* are quite honestly: ***FREAK-FREE ZONES!!!***

Telegraph Avenue, gloats the "good life" guide, is an "exhilarating place no one should miss."

If that's what it truly takes to get exhilarated in the Bog then trust me: you can miss it, all right, and not miss a frickin' thing!

PERFECT ESCAPE

"You've got them, the dreaded Visitors From Out of Town. They come into your house, take over your living room, and suddenly assume that you're the final word on everything worth seeing or doing in Berkeley. Well, the end is not at hand—you're in control. With **Guide to the Good Life** *on your side, you can impress any parent or grade-school rival."*—Guide to the Good Life in Berkeley

L et's come way down to Earth and come right out with it: anyplace, anywhere **OUT**—preferably out of this world, far, far away to the farthest galaxy to the back of beyond, beyond that is, the backward, barbaric, butt-**UGLY** Bog of Berkeley—**IS** the utmost perfect day outing!

So, you're an oh—**SO** special Cal student and you figure it's very likely you may receive and welcome with not–so–welcome arms certain out–of–town visitors whom you anxiously dread and desperately wish you could altogether avoid—typically your most unappreciated family relations or old hometown friends whom you left behind while you went off to do such supposedly great things at Cal to run back home later on to boast and gloat about—since now you somehow misguidedly think they're beneath you or you're afraid they'll somehow cause you embarrassment among your new-found, pretentiously sophisticated and pseudo-intellectual friends!

Well, grow up, get real, don't fool yourself and don't even *think* about being so self-consciously smug and self-flattering: because these very perceptive and insightful visitors, already overly familiar with the real...

you, already know full well how thankless and ungrateful you are for all the good things they did to send you to and keep you at Cal—hoping against hope to get rid of you for as long as humanly possible!—and they pay you a friendly visit now only out of some sense of indefinite responsibility for fulfilling some doubtful duty or obligation to you!

After all, before their visit's all over they also know full well that your prime objective will be to hit them up(like street vagrants)for as much handout money as you can coax, cajole and wheedle them to hand over! So if you're indeed intending to so manipulate and take undue advantage of your visiting guests by wringing from them(like street vagrants)undeserved gifts of moneyed charity then the very *least* you can do is show them an honest–to–goodness good time by mercifully taking them far, far and way, way out—**OUT** of the frickin' backward, barbaric, butt-**UGLY** Bog of Berkeley! There's absolutely **nothing** whatever worth either seeing or doing in the Bog because there's absolutely nothing whatever of any imaginable interest there! Expatriate novelist Gertrude Stein's scurrilous comment concerning Oakland applies equally if not even more aptly to the Bog: ***there is no there there!***

"Berkeley and Oakland are not on the well-beaten tourist path," the City•*Stupid* guide stupidly proclaims. "...There are no tour buses. There are no audio guides. There are no phalanxes of visitors snapping photographs of wacky bumper stickers..."

Well, with good frickin' reason: *nobody wants to go where there's no there there!*

So go to ***SAN FRANCISCO!***

CHAPTER TWO: HOVEL-HUNTING IN THE BOG

"Anyone who has ever lived in Berkeley can tell you a horror story about finding a place to live. People moan about living on friends' couches, paying $1000 a month for a 10' by 10' studio, or living in sketchy neighborhoods with gang-style shootings outside their window...The rental market in the Berkeley area...is exorbitantly expensive. This problem is made worse by the fact that recently, the vacancy rate in the area has been below 1%, and you will be competing against rich professionals for those few open spots."—Guide to the "Good Life" in Berkeley

"*A**h, Berkeley, where the coffee is rich, the conversation is deep, and the pizza is always just right—why would anyone live anywhere else?*" *stupidly spouts the* "*good life*" *guide.*

Ah, the backward, barbaric, butt-**UGLY** Bog of Berkeley—where like the lifer inmates the coffee is bitter and putrid, the thinking is warped and twisted, the conversation is misinformed and meaningless and the "ethnic food" is fake and fitted to suit American taste!

So if by chance some irrationally idiotic **RETARD** does happen to ask you for some irrationally idiotic reason—why live anyplace else?—then you might most astutely and sensibly answer with your own rhetorical question: *why the frick live there at all???* I mean, like, *what the frick for???*

There is no compellingly logical or rational reason at all for living(subsisting or stagnating)in the Bog besides being compelled to live(subsist or stagnate)there by force under the coercive threat of violent bodily harm or death! Really, the single most plausible and practical reason at all for living in the Bog is comparatively cheaper studio or "in-law" apartment rent allowing you to still live in the Bay Area close enough to enjoy and delight in the infinite delights of that magnificent City across and by the Bay: *San Francisco!* But with the discredited pretense of rent control("rent stabilization")now nicely evicted, so to speak, from the Bog(in utter disgrace!)then even that remotest of remote motives(alibis or excuses)for living in the Bog has duly faded and fast evaporated to the vanishing point! Rent control, so-called, effectively expired when vacancy control, so-called, expired: when a tenant moves out voluntarily the landlord or slumlord can jack up the rent at whim.

49

But if you're seriously bound and determined to make an arrant ass of yourself by freely suffering and enduring the prolonged pain of voluntarily living in the Bog—by choice, on purpose and of your own misguided free will—then you can at least alight there along with all the other bumbling and blundering Bog-Bugs armed with the whole truth and reality about hovel-hunting in the Bog!

Why even wastefully bother listening to horror tales about fruitlessly looking for someplace to live in the Bog when it's quite enough to know full well in the first place: ***simply living in the Bog is a perfectly horrific, horrifying and nightmarish tale of horror in and of itself???!!!***

§

LIVING IN THE NEVERENDING NIGHTMARE OF BERKELEY

I f you're damned and doomed to subsist or stagnate in the backward, barbaric, butt-***UGLY*** Bog of Berkeley for whatever apology or alibi then you should know right off that the Bog's penal camps and compounds(native captives stuck and stranded in perpetuity till doomsday kindheartedly call them "neighborhoods")spread readily to the four main points of the compass: north(the well–off and well–to–do made of money, means and living on the fat of the land high off someone else's hog!); south(the dregs of the poor and penniless, the destitute and distressed, barely surviving on the Bog's leavings and leftovers!); east(Cal campus and its hybrid, motley mixture of the prosperous and pauperized!); and west(a sprawling level spread of tediously spare sparsity!)! "There is a kind of common wisdom," the *Insider's* guide grudgingly concedes, "that neighborhoods in the Berkeley-Oakland hills are the most desirable, and that the flatlands are less so." Stuck and stranded smack dab in the middle of the whole damn, dull, drab and dreary **DUMP** is *you*—the gullible and easily gulled student or victim!

As for daily, everyday realities of subsisting and stagnating in the Bog go don't let the Bog's specious swindlers and sharpers suck you in and snare you with their trite and hackneyed euphemisms about hovel-hunting in the Bog: real hovel selections are few and far between, there are no happenin' places, there's no action to be close to and sectors of the Bog's camps and compounds known as ramshackle and run-down are out–and–out battered and dilapidated!

The south Bog in particular "is relatively run-down in areas and not one of the nicest neighborhoods in Berkeley," minces the "good life" guide.

Much if not most of the backward, barbaric, butt-**UGLY** Bog of Berkeley looks like one permanently and irrevocably barren, desolate and sterile wasteland, or even a ravaged war zone, or worse, a withered site of nuclear devastation—now overrun by scavenging poachers and ransacking sneak thieves, expertly pilfering and plundering throughout all the Bog's scraps, junk and debris whether any rioting or looting is going on or not, giving a whole new-fangled sense and meaning to the graphic expression: **GRUNGE!**

Just one day—one hour even!—of time spent wasted in the wilted and withered wasteland of Berkeley will fast make appealing and seductive enough even to the most wrongheadedly misguided among you that desperate, hurried and headlong **FLIGHT** to sweet suburbia!

Only the most tie–dyed–in–the–wool Berkeley Bog-Bugs are so oppressed, repressed and suppressed about anything and everything—as they all invariably are!—that they can't even begin to enjoy the much and mistakenly maligned and minimized pleasures and treasures of suburbia, simply because they couldn't, don't and wouldn't even know how!

As for Oakland and the rest of the entire frickin' East Bay you don't even want to go there! There's just *no there there!*

Even as it minces about Oakland's "run-down dumps in very sketchy areas," the "good life" guide cautions understatedly, "so be careful where you look...Overall, Oakland is a nice place to live, but choose your spots wisely."

Get wise, all right, and stay well out of Oakland altogether!

BLACK FLAG

WARNINGS

AGAINST

STUDENT

LIVING

ARRANGEMENTS

IN THE BOG

DORMITORIES

If you're like far too many students appear to be these days, you're obsessively in search of surrogate, substitute parents and you desperately long for the condescending paternalism of hearth and home, then by all means Cal dorms are the surest way to go: nosy busybody floor "counselors," monitors, social directors and tutors will pry and snoop into your personal lives and meddle in your personal affairs, arbitrarily and capriciously intruding and interfering whenever it's convenient, expedient or serves official university purposes—namely: to safeguard and protect the university's vested interests in exempting and releasing the university from any and all liability or responsibility whatever should anything harmful happen to happen to you while they stoop to take your money and let you live in their cramped and overcrowded prison cell block-style "units."

If you do decide to voluntarily surrender yourself to dorm authorities for detention, confinement and correction then whatever you do don't gripe and grumble childishly about the mess hall-style cafeteria food: healthful, nutritious and cheap at the price—it's one of the best and most beneficial bargains you can buy in the backward, barbaric and butt-**UGLY** Bog of Berkeley!

As the "good life" guide blusters, "...you'll find creative menus, lots of variety, and fun places to be at mealtimes."

Whoopee!!!!

COOPERATIVE STUDENT HOUSING

A nd speaking of life imprisonment if it's slavery and voluntary servitude you're after then by all means co-op housing through the *University Students Cooperative Association(USCA)*is the surest way to go: you not only pay to live in some overcrowded commune, enjoying little privacy or quiet at all, but you also pay to do your unfair share of weekly, servile housekeeping chores. Only after you've served a very lengthy prison term sentence(official translation: "seniority")and you've done your unfair share of servile dirty work can you even *think* about buying—or bribing—your way from a room and into a private co-op apartment.

HOW TO HOVEL–HUNT IN THE BOG

Even though your most ideal and imaginary hovel will truly exist only someplace, anyplace a very long way off and out of the backward, barbaric, butt-**UGLY** Bog of Berkeley you may yet misguidedly insist and persist hunting for a hovel to squat and take dying, mortal root in: it's a relatively "free" country, and it's still your privilege and prerogative to tempt fate and run the risk of utterly wasting your young life subsisting or stagnating wherever you please for better or—in this very clear-cut case—for the worst of the worse!

So if you've already made this most ill-advised and ill-made of choices then you can most definitely forget about finding your hovel through some equally imaginary housing grapevine or rumor mill(which the "good life" guide falsely claims is "particularly thick" in the Bog): the best and surest way of finding a tolerable hovel in the Bog is of course by knowing somebody who knows somebody who knows somebody else—much like finding a passable job after graduation once you've finally realized that neither merit nor even that utterly useless degree from that highly overrated diploma mill factory and inferior establishment of lower learning that just churned you(and it!)out will even help you get a job!

Early and beforehand is actually the absolute best time to wake up and let the fullest dose of real-world reality sink in, punks!

Other things you'd be most well-advised to forget and remain totally oblivious to include:

•**Finder's Fees:** selfishly advertising outright bribes of several hundred bucks to whatever crooked and greedy landlord will stoop to let you live in their dump for some exorbitant and extortionate rent only panders to and plays into the scamming hands of the shabbiest and most corrupt of landlords—much to the outright harm, hardship and disadvantage of your poorer hovel-hunting fellows!

•**Rental Services:** Oh yeah, these private, profiteering companies(like the *Berkeley Connection, E-Housing* and *Homefinders*)serve all right—both greedy landlords and slumlords alike! Offering *them* free rental listings for their private properties at *your* expense they then charge *you* a hefty monthly fee for the dubious honor and privilege of simply looking at paper printouts of those listings!

And what, pray tell, do you invariably get from those printout listings: great numbers of anonymous, nameless telephone numbers to call to hear and listen to great numbers of answering machine or voicemail messages recited by endlessly condescending voices commanding you to leave them voice-recorded messages which they, in turn, rarely if ever call back to answer or return!

Now does that sound like a nice, nifty little racket or *WHAT???!!!*

•**Realty Companies:** Come *ON!* The grudging creeps and jerk-offs at these so-called "property management" companies(*Equity Property Management, K&S Co. Inc., Red Oak Realty* and *Remax* being amongst the most notorious in the Bog)make it abun-

dantly and bluntly clear that they have no time whatever to waste by stooping to talk together with you over
the telephone about prospective rental properties let
alone about how they're far too superior to correspond
with you by exchanging letters discussing prospective
rental properties.

You can positively count on these "property manag-
ers," so-called, to do only one thing fast and furious:
promptly post an obnoxious, three-day public notice on
your dump's door to pay or quit your place should you
be but a day late in paying your rental extortion!

•**Newspaper Ads:** First off, there's absolutely no
legitimate newspapers whatever in the backward, barbaric, butt-**UGLY** Bog of Berkeley! In their place are
commercial, free, weekly, ad-glutted *stupid*-sheets
making time to run their gratuitous and self-indulgent "editorials"(no legitimate newspapers would ever
publish)solely by running in turn their endless paid per-
sonals and sex(adult–escort–massage–services)ads!

Any classified rental listing ads are placed invariably by corrupt and crooked slumlords rehashing shitty
rental properties having high tenant turnovers due to
hasty and half-baked evictions. Either that or a big
bunch of Bog-Bug household cronies and groupies are
looking to lure unsuspecting, conformist-type dupes
into their pseudo-intellectually elitist and exclusive fold
to help pay as fellow clan members their monthly mort-
gage—but only should they first pass certain arbitrary
and capricious personality, mind-controlling, thought-
policed and puppet-ically correct philosophy tests!

HOTELS, MOTELS, GRADUATION AND THE "BIG GAME" IN THE BOG

I f you've passed with flying colors your mostly worthless courses and exams to the profitless point of actually graduating from Cal: congratulations on successfully undertaking and completing a most **MONUMENTAL** waste of youthful time, effort, energy and expense!

If for entertainment and excitement you feel forced to go to the ever-so-predictable "Big Game" the week before Thanksgiving which Cal invariably loses to Stanford then you desperately need to **GET A LIFE!** since your existing one is as good as dead as *the DEAD!* The Berkeley **BASHER** says: *Frick* Monday(or Friday)Night Football! Make a night of *fricking* your neglected wife or girlfriend instead! You'll have a far better fun time!

Though the City•*Stupid* guide apologizes that the Cal Golden Bears football team has "suffered from a revolving door of coaches," the *Insider's* guide is a lot more forthright: "...the football team has had a miserable record of late, winning only one game in 2001...Cal's Golden Bears football team has had a miserable record the past few seasons...They are near the bottom of the Pac 10 each year. They lost 12 consecutive games in the 2000–2001 seasons, including the shameful 54–27 loss to USC..." So only a "miserable" **LOSER** would go so habitually to watch this "miserable" team **LOSE** so miserably, monotonously and redundantly!

If you're so thoughtless and inconsiderate that you'd even halfway seriously consider lodging your not–so–valued–or–cared–for friends and family relations in any of those dingy, low-life motels doing business all along either San Pablo or University Avenues then at least show enough common courtesy and decency to warn your unwary victims to be alert and on their guard against the no end of holdup muggers, robbers, drive–by or gangland, execution–style shooters, pimps and prostitutes swarming like preying locusts over those two strips at night!

Or at least caution them that their next-door motel neighbor could very well be some "sketchy" criminal suspect some cop arrested and actually took into custody, but being too timid to book the suspect into jail on shaky probable cause, handed the suspect a city-paid room "voucher" to put up the suspect at your motel instead! *Charming!*

One such suspect resort hostel is the hot–pink exteriored *Flamingo Motel* on University Avenue which the "good life" guides minces "is as scary on the inside as the outside with its chipped, bright pink paint."

"The facilities are basic, a little worn at the edges, and a little musty—just a bed, dresser, TV, and shower," minces the City•*Stupid* guide. "In other cases(like that of the hot pink *Flamingo Motel*)," the *Insider's* guide apologizes, "lodgings are not listed because they look a little old and tired or just downright shabby...For the most part the smaller motels in the area fell below our standards."

You can't whitewash wretched blight—even hot pink—with apologetic understatement!

A supposed *"Bonus"* of staying at the so-called *French Hotel* in the north Bog, according to the equally apologetic "good life" guide, is its adjoining cafe espresso bar—reputedly a "favorite gathering spot for North Berkeleyites."

"The funky cafe," eulogizes the City•*Stupid* guide, "is its heart and soul and *echt* Berkeley—especially from seven to nine at night when the neighborhood crowd spills out to the sidewalk tables and the din of intellectual discussion is, well, truly French."

"The cafe," likewise eulogizes the *Insider's* guide, "is also one of Berkeley's most famous spots, an intellectual's hangout where cultural relativism or Cechen politics may be discussed over lattes and cappuccinos on the sidewalk out front. If you're on your own, read *Le Monde* to look ever so cool."

Two extremes at opposite ends of the same spectrum: the *Flamingo Motel* epitomizes the height of Bog **denial** while the *French Hotel* epitomizes the height of Bog **pretention!**

Now look, it's most likely going to be too friggin' cold to sit outside at smutty sidewalk tables in the first friggin' place. And if you impossibly think that mixing and mingling with the mostly discontented, disgruntled, disillusioned, frustrated pseudo-intellectual and altogether **PSYCHONEUROTIC** "North Berkeleyites" habitually haunting the *French Hotel* cafe in the so-called "gourmet ghetto" somehow perversely adds some sort of big *"BONUS"*(as the "good life" guide blusters)to the monotonous visit you've forced yourself to pay to the backward, barbaric, butt-**UGLY** Bog of Berkeley then you're doubtless much too far gone and hopelessly beyond any and all help or hope!

And may God have boundless mercy on your poor, pathetic soul!

JOSEPH COVINO JR

TANGIBLE TIP

"Renting is a touchy issue in Berkeley," the City•*Stupid* guide apologizes understatedly. "Tenants are so active as a political force that a Rent Control Board is required to adjudicate disputes. Its proceedings are of such widespread interest that they are televised every week on Berkeley cable channel 25. There are 24,455 rental units in Berkeley. The median monthly rent for an apartment is a steep $638."(That was circa *2000*).

If while hovel-hunting in the backward, barbaric, butt-**UGLY** Bog of Berkeley you do happen to stumble on some captivating hovel that intrigued or invited your interest enough to excite your desire to rent the hovel then you'd be wise and well-advised to go first(before shelling out any rent money or deposits)to the offices of the City of Berkeley's *Rent Stabilization Program* to carefully check out and look over the public file(catalogued by street address)on the prospective rental property you have a mind to squat on. Once you've studiously read and reviewed this file—conscientious student that you are!—you'll know and be far more aware and informed about the property's officially recorded and documented history. Then you'll find out, among other helpful and practical things, what the rental unit's true lawful rent ceiling(if any)is—to prevent some slumlord from illegally rent-gouging! But even more importantly you'll learn what exactly you'll be exposing and laying yourself open to by way of the landlord's chronicled line of conduct(or misconduct!)and ways of doing business(or monkey business!)!

Renter **BEWARE!**

Two to three months ahead of time during the rental downtime periods of February–March and October–November when fewer people are searching for housing is the prime time for hovel-hunting in the Bog!

"If you show up in Berkeley expecting to find an ideal apartment in a day or two," exhorts the "good life" guide, "you may find yourself sleeping in People's Park."

As enchanting a prospect as camping out on the resplendent plot of People's Park truly is at least the guide got *that* right!

Now on to how the "good life" guide admonishes students about *cars* in a manner that its elitist "editors" would never dare condescend to Cal campus professors, "professionals" or other assorted members of the Bog's titled aristocratic gentry:

*"Owning a car in Berkeley is often more of a headache than a convenience, especially since the city is small enough that you can walk or bike to most neighborhoods...**register your car** at Parking and Transportation, which involves purchasing a yearly parking permit, although they are really attempting to make it very difficult to have a car at school with almost no parking and other assorted trials and tribulations involving your car—think bicycles and mass transit."*

Tell **them** to think bikes and mass transit!

CHAPTER THREE: CARS, COPS & MAKING THE BOG SAFE FOR CELIBACY

"Perhaps you've already heard the horror stories about the DMV—long lines, endless forms, bored and condescending staff. Well, it's all true. Going to the DMV is a long, complicated and exceedingly frustrating exercise in bureaucracy."—Guide to the "Good Life" in Berkeley

BITS OF THE BOG

You can self-inflict on yourself some severe automotive pain, distress, hardship and trouble should you join the *California State Automobile Association*—or the California Mutation of the *American Automobile Association(AAA)*—more notoriously known as *Triple A.*

Whatever else this automotive club stands for or hawks about("emergency road service" and trip maps)to people at large just know and be actuely aware of this: shyster lawyers advertising on late-night TV solicit prospective legal clients for purposes of suing the *Triple A* in civil court for chronically and habitually rejecting expensive club member insurance claims and stubbornly resisting to settle and pay up on costly claims—until *forced* to do so by a court-ordered judgment awarded through a civil action lawsuit.

Don't get conned like a chump with that come-on about supposedly "free" car-towing service for club members either: yeah, it's "free" all right—within an extremely finite and limited(translation: *short!*)distance. Towing your disabled motor vehicle farther outside and beyond that distance for any long-range or even reasonably lengthy distance will cost you an unreasonably expensive and excessive base–and–per–mileage fee!

It calls to mind the idiocy of that clodhead cyclist-terrorist who rudely pedals his lubberly bike onto the crowded sidewalk, bowling along and plowing into people, hauling that cumbrous and bulky buggy displaying that boldly emblazoned sign—*ONE LESS CAR*—when it should really read: *ONE MORE **IDIOT!!!!***

DEPARTMENT OF MOTOR VEHICLES
(DMV)

This road gang of legalized highway robbers, blackmailers, extortionists, thieves and swindlers would be more aptly re-named the **DDMV**(*Draconian Department of Motor Vultures*) or even more accurately the **DHR**(*Department of Highway Robbery*)!—take your pick!

No end of creeping, overlong, snail-paced lines and no end of numberless forms to fill out are the very *least* of the untold difficulty, disappointment, discouragement, dissatisfaction and outright distress that you'll be forced to face each and every time you set unsuspecting foot inside the *DMV's* dictatorial and demonic den! Going there is to suffer an infinitely torturous and tyrannical bureaucratic exercise in utter futility and frustration!

Don't let yourself be fooled by the misleadingly humanoid appearance of the *DMV's* ruthless henchmen and hirelings either: those indifferently bored, boorish, brazen and condescendingly rude and obnoxious lieutenants(deviously misnamed "customer service reps")aren't humans in monkey suits! Quite the contrary they're brainless *monkeys in human suits!* Their robotic bearing and demeanor are more android than anthropoid! And their sole mechanical, pre-activated and pre-programmed purpose shown and proved by their legalized criminal method–of–operation is: to legally bilk and milk you of as many of your hard-earned bucks(by fleecing you for exorbitant—and extortionate—sums of money for vehicle registrations, smog certificates and extravagantly excessive state sales taxes!)as they possibly can!

JOSEPH COVINO JR

TANGIBLE(DMV)TIPS

Don't even register your car in the frickin' state of California at all if you can help it: remain instead a perennial out–of–state tourist or visitor indefinitely, never sticking on your car any tell-tale signs or tokens(like local stickers or parking permits)of your residency, never admitting to anyone to even being in the tyrannical state for more than ten days! Or keep your car registered in somebody else's name out–of–state. Or do as I do: drive other people's cars(if you're trustworthy enough)or simply don't drive at all—a car registered in California is nothing but a devious lever the state and its imperious parasites exploit as a strong-arm tactic to twist your arm to extort from you whatever fines or fees they shake you down for.

If you do decide to "trade" in your out–of–state driver's license for a California driver's license, but for some reason your home-state one holds some sentimental value for you(like your dated photograph!)and you'd care to keep it, then whatever you do don't voluntarily hand it over to the listless, mindless *monkey in the human suit* slouching across the counter from you: for without giving any notice or warning whatever the manic, maniacal *monkey* will stupidly slice your other driver's license, cutting it in half before discarding the severed pieces! Frickin' ***IDIOTS, MORONS AND RETARDS!!!***

And whatever you do never, ever smile for your California driver's license photograph: instead scowl with the strongest and most caustic contempt and disgust possible to let each and every cop who stops you on the road know precisely and how resentfully you scorn and spurn them!

PARKING AND PUBLIC-ABUSING TRANSPORTATION IN THE BOG

K eeping and keeping up a car in the backward, barbaric, butt-*UGLY* Bog of Berkeley is typically more than an annoying inconvenience or a bothersome nuisance: more often than not it's an out–and–out baneful burden to bear!

Well aside from all those absurdly asinine, inane, idiotic, imbecilic and moronic *"traffic diverters"*(to say nothing of all those silly and stupid *"speed bumps"*)—hideously huge and ugly solid concrete barriers—scattered vexingly everywhere and deviously designed to obnoxiously and outrageously block, detour and delay thru traffic from deviating anywhere throughout the Bog's backward, barbaric and butt-*UGLY* penal camps and compounds(otherwise known as "neighborhoods")there's the Bog's insidiously involuntary system of systematic taxation without representation: despotically-enforced parking tickets!

Except during those hours roughly between around dusk to dawn—unless of course you're a proud, private property landowner(and member of the titled aristocratic gentry)owning a parking garage as well—there's absolutely no place wherever in the whole backward, barbaric, butt-*UGLY* Bog of Berkeley where you can park your car for *free:*

•If you live as a renter in a penal camp or compound then you *have* to buy from the Bog an annual parking permit to stick onto your car—or else get fined by parking ticket!

•If you simply drive to pay a social call to a penal camp or compound as a free-wheeling visitor then you *have* to buy from the Bog a one-day, three-day or two-week parking permit—or else get fined by parking ticket!

•If you simply park briefly for more than a mere two hours in a penal camp or compound as a visitor—you can get fined by parking ticket!

•If you park in a penal camp or compound on the wrong side of the street at the wrong time of day or night during an arbitrarily and capriciously scheduled "street-cleaning"—you can get fined by parking ticket!

•If you park too long by the wrong-colored street curb—or in a marked street space by a parking meter that runs swiftly out of time before shooting up its ominous red flag!—then you can get fined by parking ticket!

•If you feed a parking meter past its initially allotted time you can *still* get fined by frickin' parking ticket!

And of course if you collect enough despotically-enforced parking tickets then you can get your car **towed away!**

If for whatever trumped-up alibi under the "law"—a state vehicular "code" drawn up and drafted by autocratic bureaucrats, *not* your elected, lawmaking representatives—the cops order your car towed away here's how the legalized auto theft–and–extortion ring works in the backward, barbaric, butt-**UGLY** Bog of Berkeley:

•First the Bog's cops order your car to be towed away and impounded. Beware and be forewarned: even Cal's campus cops can be in on the ring and can order your car to be towed—even if it's parked someplace *off*-campus outside their habitual, prey-pursuing territorial jurisdiction.

After all, money's money. And since money's what the game of running a legalized, organized crime ring's all about—that is, extracting and extorting money from *you!*—their state-awarded authority lets Cal cops loose to run amuck ticketing or towing cars *all over* the frickin' Bog! So take warning: no place in the Bog's "safe" or secure, for sure, for parking your car unless it's on private property—and even that's not foolproof secure!

•Next, you'll have to confront those ruthless monkeys in mortal suits at either the **DMV** or the Bog's very own ***"Parking Collection Bureau"*** as part of the Bog's rampant, legalized extortion racket pipeline: here you'll first be legally blackmailed to **PAY** and settle whatever picayunish parking or traffic ticket fines that petty, ticket-quota-happy, penny-ante police have hit you up with—just to buy off from them a proof–of–purchase *"clearance."*

•Then you'll have to deal with those monkeys in mortal suits manning the barricades at the Bog's(or Cal's)forbidding, hostile and onerous police station. Of whatever cowardly and craven stripe the cops are you'll next be legally blackmailed to **PAY** even more money to buy off from *them* a car-towing *"release."* There two imperious female *monkeys in mortal suits* will stay stubbornly *seated* and yell at *you* from inside their airtight bulletproof glass box, ordering *you* to speak up louder through the small speaker slot supposedly because they can't hear *you* speaking; but actually because they outright refuse to budge and move their fat and lazy-ass butts—irrevocably *riveted and rooted* to their cushioned chairs!—from their fixed and irrevocably immovable positions! Frickin' ***INCREDIBLE!***

•Finally, you'll have to face even more monkeys in mortal suits at the treacherous towing company itself: the notorious ***HUSTEAD'S!***(or whichever one has the latest criminal franchise).

Running in cahoots and collusion with the Bog's petty, penny-ante police—conniving and conspiring together under some exclusive and nefarious franchise-fee scheme—***Hustead's*** sticks(shafts!)you not just for its exorbitant(extortionate!)towing fee but also for its daily-imposed "storage" charge for as long as your car's impounded—or until it's officially confiscated and seized to be disposed of on the police auction block!

All during the time that this entire legalized auto theft–blackmail–and–extortion racket unfolds it's *your* legally-owned car that's held up for forcible ransom!

Take some small heart, comfort and consolation though in these factual and most gratifying and satisfying incidents:

•The Bog's *"Parking Collection Bureau"* was forced to move underground to the hellish and nethermost basement of the base city hall building after being run out of its old building by irate victims repeatedly smashing and shattering its front plate glass windows! ***HA! HA! HA!***

•In the powerful, pounding and pulverizing earthquake of 1989 ***Hustead's*** exploded and burned beautifully! Ablaze and in flames the building went up in gloriously soaring billows of smoke—as if by some justly punishing act of God for all the financial pain, suffering, hardship and misery this entire legalized scam inflicts on the poorest and most impoverished of its victims!

Sometimes there are indeed some poetically just deserts in the world however small or scarce!

If none of this were enough: if at anytime during your car-towing ordeal you happen to decry or otherwise raise your objecting voice in protest against this whole corrupt and crooked setup then it's highly likely that some jowly, beer-bellied, paunchy, paper-pushing, do-nothing **DESK JOCKEY** of a cop—lying low in hiding at the police station with no major felony arrests to his credit—will pompously presume to condescendingly lecture you that **HE** pays all **HIS** bills and never gets **HIS** car towed off!

Well, let's just take a good, hard look at this inept, ineffectual, hammy-handed pig–in–blue: he slouches there, watching the creeping clock and wasting away his life in his worthless job, doing the dirty work of his deadbeat employer: a "city" deep in debt from running in the **RED**—an extravagant, overindulgent luxury none of the rest of us mere mortals can even afford much less get away with!

By **RIGHT** this blubber-faced, blubbering pig doesn't even deserve to get paid the floated and unsecured paycheck he didn't even earn or merit—much less the frickin' free parking space job-perk he's favored with!

Point **IS**: this sloven slob of a piggy will be paying his bills like everybody else when he pays **FOR** a daily parking space **FEE** like everybody else!

"Parking in Berkeley..." cautions the City•*Stupid* guide, "can be frustrating because many of the lots around the university require stickers. Some of the city's downtown and campus lots use an antiquated system in which you must fold up dollar bills like origami and squeeze them into miniscule slots. Others take only quarters, and still others take nothing at all(anti-meter guerrillas have decapitated them). The latest innovation is single meters that cover five spaces..."

BRAVO to all meter-decapitating meter **GUER-RILLAS!**

BOG-BUG COPS: ROUSTERS, SEX-BUSTERS AND VOYEURS!

ersonally, I'd just **LOVE** to square off one–on–one with any willing Bog cop—especially one credited with writing the most traffic tickets and making the fewest felony arrests—in a physical bout of fisticuffs for the pure **PLEASURE** of it. But as we all know most cops are power-tripping control freaks acting much like lawless street gangs: both run in cowardly packs to prey relentlessly on those they perceive as too weak and defenseless to fight back. Both hide most cowardly behind weapons their victims can't or typically don't carry.

And in a very telling way cops are far more cowardly and corrupt since they also hide behind badges and unequal laws giving them unjust license and immunity to abuse(and misuse)authority as well as to commit even the pettiest of crimes forbidden to the rest of us: like cruising like sharks those red curb zones to exact taxation–by–traffic tickets for stopping and parking in to use the very same bank automated teller machines(*ATMs*)**THEY** do!(Just stake out Bank of America or Wells Fargo Bank any Friday evening in the Bog and catch them!).

If you think that's too harsh, or worse, misguidedly swallow that propagandistic slogan about *"protecting and serving the community"* then just bend your brain a bit and ask yourself honestly these few simple questions:

•When was the last time you were **ANYWHERE** served much less protected by a cop?

•When have you **EVER** been helped—not **HARASSED** and **HAMPERED**—by a cop?

•When, for that matter, have you ever met a cop showing even an **ATTITUDE** for helping much less protecting or serving you?

Well, then, *I rest my case!*

In the backward, barbaric, butt-**UGLY** Bog of Berkeley the petty, penny ante and utterly useless police **EXCEL** supremely at rousting(typically with up to five or more *"back-up"* reinforcements)the homeless street people, rousting students riding bikes or motor scooters without their token "safety" lights and ritually cruising *"downtown"* bank ATMs on busy, overcrowded Friday evenings in hot pursuit of tired working stiffs making quick stops in red curb zones to briefly park and deposit their paltry paychecks!(the cops do the same thing with their city-subsidized paychecks with immunity *and* impunity!).

So if ever you're confronted with a seriously violent criminal—mugger, robber, rapist, murderer or any other life-threatening assailant—then don't even bother wasting your time trying to call some Bog-Bug cop-thug for help: if the "emergency" dispatcher doesn't tell you that Bog-Bug cops are either *"too busy"* or just *"don't have the time"* to respond to your particular life–and–death emergency the cops will most likely deliberately dawdle and take their sweet time in getting to your crime scene—since they know full well that if they hang back and play for time long enough your attacker will have plenty of time to make their getaway!

Now, no end of violent crime goes down in the Bog's penal camps and compounds, not only because Bog-Bug cops stay mostly in hiding to purposely avoid any serious crimebusting, but also because they fail and neglect to even go into those "neighborhoods" to cruise and patrol for any real criminal activity. Instead, they rove the Bog's main avenues and "corridors" on the blood-sniffing trail of traffic ticket victims!

And if they're not roaming the traffic ticket, *mother lode road* then there's likely only one other spot in the whole wide Bog where they're actually on duty and on the job: prowling, stalking and voyeuring in the Bog's several ***LOVER'S LANES!***

And just so you won't jump to any rash conclusions and wrongheadedly think that there's absolutely nothing whatever in the Bog worth liking or praising I'll confess right off that I dearly ***LOVE*** and revel in making love at night with my warm and willing sweatheart in a comfortable car having a beautiful, brilliantly panoramic view of *San Francisco Bay* along with its splendid and scintillating scenery! Marveling at the boundless beauty of both her and our sublime surroundings has more to do of course with admiring and appreciating the natural form, features and charm of creation than with the Bog itself. But even so I could hardly deny the incredibly breathtaking and spectacular vistas that can be ecstatically enjoyed from *Inspiration Point* in *Tilden Regional Park*, the *Lawrence Hall of Science*, the *Berkeley Hills*, volcanic *Indian Rock Park* or even the Bog's very own landfill(no, it's *not* natural coastline!) *Marina!* Forget nearby *Aquatic Park* as well unless you fondly relish the rank stench of raw sewage which permeates it!

"Perched on the hill high above the UC Berkeley campus," the *Insider's* guide gushes about the *Lawrence Hall of Science*, "the view from the parking lot and the plaza in front of the building alone makes a trip there worthwhile..." Well, what the frick good is a grand view if at dusk some impotent Cal campus cop attempting to enlarge his little wick by wielding his nightstick comes along acting like a prick???

Outrageously though the Bog's petty, penny ante and utterly useless police get their ecstatic kicks and cheap thrills by diligently and devoutly haunting and stalking each and every last one of these potentially romantic spots in search of steamy car windows and coddling couples—likely their sole source of orgasmic pleasure and sexual gratification! Misery loves company: so since the Bog-Bug cops are getting **NONE** they naturally feel uncontrollably compelled to disturb and perturb those gloriously getting a **LOT**—of **HOT**—because they're **NOT!!!**

So take heed: if you drive to any of these wonderful places in amorous hopes of even feasting on a magnificent view much less on each other then you can dependably count on the Bog-Bug cops to feel intractably duty-bound to go out of their way to do their very best to disrupt and **SCREW UP** your opportunity to get rapturously and sumptuously screwed! So take some heart—and benefit—from these:

TANGIBLE TIPS

You're stuck in your car with your fervid, nubile and intensely sensual friend or lover only you've absolutely no privacy at your place since your resolute roommate wouldn't leave if your walls were crumbling down around your heads! So what do you do, knowing full well that the Bog-Bug cops are out prowling all the Bog's lover's lanes in hot pursuit of voyeurized victims?

Easy: head for some good head in the dark, narrow and hilly streets of the north Bog or even nearby *Kensington* where the peaceful and quiet neighborhood parking niches are shaded, shadowed and overspread by woodsy trees and foliage! There you'll hear nothing but your lover's ecstatic cries and, apart from her desirous eyes, flushed face and supple flesh you'll see nothing in the soft and soothing lamplight except perhaps some stray, passing deer, foraging and pricking up their curious ears.

Or if you're stuck together on foot then just *foot it* across Cal campus to the ever so many erotic and passionate spots among the picturesque and closely clustered eucalyptus groves(hint: the very best spots are around hedge-heavy **Evans Hall**, the oak-studded **Faculty Glade** and the woodsy *north* fork of Strawberry Creek)or beyond to the sweet-scented shrubbery of the **Berkeley Rose Garden** or across the street to its facing and densely wooded **Cordonices Park**. Downstream is **Live Oak Park** with its thinner thickets! Steer clear of the **Eucalyptus Grove** proper at the foot of Cal campus where marauding Cal campus cop-voyeurs have gone prowling and stalking to get their dud rocks off catching amorous nude students burning up the underbrush! Otherwise: *Enjoy!* But if you do brave **Aquatic Park** as one of *Nature Company*-founder Priscilla Wrubel's "top 10 ways to get in touch with nature" you'll likely get more in touch with your *FECAL* than your feminine side!

METER MAIDS
AND
PARTING CHEAP SHOTS
AT THE BOG

Tragically every climax has its anticlimax—like the Bog's meter maids constantly complaining about getting hassled by the common citizens in the Bog *they* constantly badger and harass! And so these exceptionally exasperating Bog-Bugs should get hassled: *they* pay court to and do the dirty work of a corrupt system and *deserve* to go to the dogs!

Every single day the Bog operates in debt, in the red and in the hole, writing bad checks and spending money it doesn't have with a daily deficit—something the rest of us can hardly afford much less get away with! But Bog bosses expect *us* to pick up the tab for their incompetence and irresponsibility by imposing on us what amounts to an unjust and regressive sales tax scheme: flat-fee parking or traffic tickets that proportionately hurt poorer people due to their lesser ability to pay. By all *RIGHT* meter maids shouldn't even get their unearned, counterfeit and delinquent paychecks!

So while the Bog deficit-spends at our expense it preaches pompously about parking violators *"breaking the law,"* raising *"revenues"* through parking tickets and prompting *"turnover"* among *"downtown"* visitors. Okay, let's talk **turnover**: how about doing away with meter maids altogether and putting their paychecks into human-helping programs for the homeless, unemployed or working poor whom the Bog screws over with its regressive parking taxation program?

One sure way to motivate this more desirable **turnover** is to look out for those parking meter red flags while you walk those Bog byways and put in some coins—yes, even if it's not for your own car!—and turn those meters **OVER** so they can't get ticketed! Then you help your fellow neighbor, strike a well-deserved blow against corruption and graft and **PAY BACK** a corrupt *"city"* for precisely what it puts out day after insufferable day!

And whenever you can do it while some brazen-faced meter maid is right in your face ticketing some car—that's when it's the most **FUN!**

§

So let's close taking note of some salient points:

•Redundant mention is often made of the Oakland Coliseum **BART**(*Bay Area Rapid Transit*)station.

Well, if you're riding the train to this particular station for the express and wishful purpose of transferring to an **Alameda-Contra Costa Transit**(*AC Transit*)bus, supposedly servicing Alameda County in which the Bog is deeply embedded, then all I can say to you is: **FAT, FRICKIN' CHANCE!**

"If you plan to get around by public transportation,"

the City•*Stupid* guide falsely claims, "you can catch buses to the Coliseum BART station, which arrive every 10 minutes, at the entrances to both terminals."

Yeah, right. In this "neighborhood" these particular barbarous and obnoxious bus drivers drive at their own pleasure and convenience and no one else's—meaning, more specifically, at your displeasure and inconvenience: typically they simply and slowly pass **BY** bus-stop signs, glancing around quickly for waiting passengers. And if they don't see a certain quota and quorum standing stiffly there on the watch then they roll on by without stopping and drive off just as quickly—leaving you enraged and infuriated to wait for the next bus(and the next so on and so forth!)on the very same route to repeat the maddening cycle all over again! It's enough to drive even the mildest and most mild-mannered of passengers stark, staring *MAD!!!*

•False claim is also made that you invariably need to make a needless *reservation*("Reservations are mandatory," spouted the "good life" guide)to ride any number of private shuttle vans(like the *BayPorter Express*)offering door–to–door pickup and delivery from the Bog to surrounding area airports!

"The only real drawback," grumbles the City•*Stupid* guide, "is the fact that these vehicles pick up and drop off other passengers, so you may have to wake up extra early to make sure you don't miss your flight."

BULL! Think *AGAIN*: it may very well even be shuttle company "policy" for passengers to make advance reservations but if you simply show up at just about any time of the day at a one-stop shuttle pickup at either of the Bog's two traditional *hotels*(the *Durant* or the *Shattuck*, which is most conveniently but a block from the "downtown" *BART* station)—with or without bags or baggage—waving your colorful greenbacks:

do you really believe these overworked and underpaid drivers(typically friendly if frazzled Latinos looking to please!)will actually turn you down and pass up earning more money since they're charging a reduced per-head fare already for vans that are rarely if ever full with riders???!!! Now **REALLY!**

•"**Bay Area Rapid Transit**," the "good life" guide adulates, "better known as **BART**, is a blessing for active Berkeley residents."

More like a **curse**—and a grievously **evil** one at that!

Those lazy, loafing, do-nothing slackers and shirkers(otherwise known as *station agents*)"working" for *BART*—more *monkeys in mortal suits* making up perhaps merely a single link in the food chain below that occupied by *DMV* agents—act pretty much the same all over: they're imperiously and indifferently crass, cross, crude, rude and obnoxious! Shell-shocked as they are they're as ever ready to *"call the po-lice"* on anyone and everyone as they are to walk off the job and go on strike, leaving untold daily commuters stuck and stranded while demanding undeserved raises in pay and benefits they neither earn nor merit simply because they offer the least customer-friendly, least helpful but most hindering "service" in Bay Area public transit(*AC Transit* runs them a close second!). They simply have no time to be bothered by you as a paying patron—in spite of the fact that the high-priced fares you're paying unduly support their extravagant *union* wages and benefits—and they never let you forget it because by countless ways and means they constantly let you know it! It's little wonder they post profuse signs threatening stiff fines and lengthy prison terms for assaulting and battering these *slime-buckets* since they habitually and frequently provoke potential assaults by passengers purely by their typical incivility!

"Unlike subways in some metropolitan areas," at least admits the *Insider's* guide, "the *BART* system tends to run in single linear paths...Station agents do not handle any kind of money." They handle or deal with little else either.

"Every BART train includes maps that make transferring easy," puffs the City•*Stupid* guide.

Since there are only *five* East Bay lines in the entire system transferring *should* be easy and shouldn't demand maps!

Unknown to everyone except the **IDIOTS, MORONS** and **RETARDS** who run the system and ride herd over the hordes riding it is the secret solution to that incessant esoteric mystery: why does *BART* burn itself out making the simple act of transferring between train lines so extremely and exceptionally difficult and troublesome?

Frickin' **COMMON SENSE** should tell anyone that since passengers can both embark and disembark from any platform on any line in the system they can likewise logically "transfer"(within certain train schedule or time limitations)from any platform on any line in the system—otherwise nobody in the frickin' system could get to any destination they were bound for!

In spite of that fact **BART** functionaries will irrationally and stubbornly insist—against all rational reason or logic—that pre-programmed passengers simply must of necessity officially "transfer" at either the *12th Street City Center* or *MacArthur* stations in Oakland in the East Bay.

Let me briefly demonstrate how ridiculously absurd that irrational obstinacy really is: a near riot among meddling busybodies once nearly ensued when I affirmed for an inquiring tourist that he could indeed board from the eastbound platform in San Francisco a *Dublin/Pleasanton* train to get to the backward, barbaric, butt-**UGLY** Bog of Berkeley!

Conventionally, pre-programmed **BART** dictate would demand that you board at a City platform either an eastbound *Richmond*(if direct trains with stops in the *Bog* were running)or an eastbound *Pittsburg/Bay Point* train with an official "transfer" at either *12th Street City Center* or *MacArthur* station in Oakland.

An eastbound *Dublin/Pleasanton* train once across the underwater transbay tube would unduly deviate and turn off—*south*bound—and so divert from any *north*bound course to the Bog!

True, **IDIOTS, MORONS, and RETARDS**: but all you have to do is disembark from the *Dublin/Pleasanton* train at the *un*-official *Lake Merritt* "transfer" station in Oakland—just a single station *briefly removed*(if just slightly *south*ward)from the official *12th Street City Center* "transfer" station(also in Oakland)—and embark on the very next Fremont/*Richmond* train right and straight to the frickin' Bog!

In fact, it might just benefit you better—not to mention *faster*—if you were stuck in the City waiting for an eastbound train to the *Bog* and the *Dublin/Pleasanton* train happened to arrive *first* and *before* the next *Richmond* or *Pittsburg/Bay* Point trains(which can run up to *20* minutes apart!)arrived!

Point is: you can still "transfer" from any platform on any line in the entire **BART** system and you needn't deviate, divert or otherwise detour exclusively to either the *12th Street City Center* or *MacArthur* stations in Oakland just to officially "transfer"—unless of course you're just another brainless, mindless, unthinking, pre-programmed, robotic automaton!

To get wherever you're going in and around the

Bay by train, then, remember to beneficially bend your **BART** brain!

What even BART's most rabid defenders won't readily let on to newcomers: the entire shitty system shuts completely down by a little past Midnight at the latest.

"Perhaps the only drawback to the Berkeley/Oakland nightlife scene is the way the sidewalks are pretty much rolled up by midnight," admits even the City•*Stupid* guide. "If you're into late nights, you may be disappointed."

Whatever you do don't dawdle to take that last train from the City to the East Bay unless you absolutely have to. Otherwise if you have to transfer you'll get unduly delayed and stuck at that frickin' anal **MacArthur** station—held hostage against your will without any warning whatever—for upwards of a full half hour while the equally anal **BART** cops barge through from car to car to roust any dozing or snoozing passengers before those last trains are finally "released" from their forced and involuntary captivity.

At the system's nightly shut-down it's funny how *all kinds* of anal cops congregate there like they're at some cop clambake! But if you're physically assaulted once you're on the move by one of the many violence-prone hoodlums haunting that last **Richmond** train the operator reached by intercom will act deaf, dumb and **RETARDED** in response to your call for assistance and no anal cops will be found to lend you any aid!

And due solely to its destination it's no wonder that the **Richmond** is the dirtiest, filthiest, grimiest and smuttiest line in the entire frickin' system!

•If any of you hale and hearty young people out there have to ride a frickin' **MUNI** bus from the San Francisco *Powell Street* **BART** station at Fourth and Market Streets rather than stride a short seven lousy blocks to get to the **CalTrain** terminal at Fourth and Townsend Streets then I feel seriously sorry for you and strongly suggest that you give it up now and take up recuperative residence at your nearest convalescence home!

RE-JECTS:
WEATHER & DIVERSITY

To falsely—and foolishly—claim that the weather in the backward, barbaric and butt-**UGLY** Bog of Berkeley is neither too hot nor too cold(that it's *just* right!)is a fabulous and fantastic **FLIGHT OF SHEER FANCY, SO FLIGHTY** and **SO FANCIFUL** that it **FLIES** far beyond mere daydreaming or indulging in reverie: such self-deluding denial and **FANTASY** borders on the very brink of utter **HALLUCINATION** if not out–and–out **DE-LIRIUM**—unless of course you're a frickin' **COCK-ROACH!!!**

Lukewarm at best it's simply never, **EVER** hot in the Bog! But even so native Bog-Bugs frenziedly FREAK OUT and go into uncontrolled HYSTERICS—if not outright CONVULSIONS—should the outdoor temperature even DARE to rise even the slightest notch above 70°F, conjuring up illusive visions of an imminent **HEAT-WAVE!!!**

So if nothing else let's at least get this straight: just two(2!)temperatures exist(and persist)in the Bog: **COLD** and **COLDER!!!** Claiming anything else is a mere figment of somebody's very overactive, overreaching, overwrought and truth-distorting imagination! Like, if diehard wind-surfers fitted out in wet-suits or their landlubber counterparts shivering and shuddering in their winter clothing in the middle of the so-called frickin' summer aren't a surefire tipoff then you sorely need to get a frickin' ***CLUE!!!*** "Unwarned tourists," admits even the City•*Stupid* guide, "can be seen shivering in their shorts and T-shirts."

Then take heed: after six o'clock in the frickin' evening as the Bog's colder temperatures typically plunge to their coldest levels ***BUNDLE UP WELL***—unless of course you perversely relish perishing with cold by tempting fate by risking pneumonia! Set even your biggest toe in any body of water in the Bog and you risk suffering ***HYPOTHERMIA!***

The East Bay, claims the specious City•*Stupid* guide, "is a paradigm of temperate climate" while the *Insider's* guide stupidly alludes to *"microclimates."* By that they contrive to perpetuate the persistent fabricated myth that a "Mediterranean climate," so-called, prevails in the Bay Area and that the weather's supposedly "warmer" in the "valley" than in the Bog which in turn is supposedly "warmer" than it is barely across the Bay in San Francisco!

Yeah, right! The unbearable and unendurable naked truth is: being compelled to wrap up in winter clothing at the height of the so-called "summer" to watch the July 4th fireworks from *anywhere* in the Bay Area— whether the Bog, the City or even the Valley—is nothing less than downright and outright ***OBSCENE!!!***

§

Of all its typically trite and hackneyed buzzwords ***DIVERSITY*** ranks high among the Bog's most pretentious platitudes: for the Bog's most pretentious pretenders look on all those supposedly ethnically and multi-culturally ***DIVERSE*** *"people of color"*(*colored people* in reverse!)as some aberrant and abnormal ***ANOMALY*** of freakish

NOVELTY to marvel at and write home about rather than as equal, admirable and noble *HUMAN* peers to consort, fraternize, socialize and keep company with!

Such canting *HYPOCRISY* is shameless and unforgivable!

"Berkeley is a city of unexpected diversity," Malcolm Margolin over-exaggerates for *Visit Berkeley: The Official Visitors Guide.*

"Diverse," the City•*Stupid* guide cants, "is the politically correct but paltry description usually given to the population of the East Bay."

What the pretentiously politically correct really mean by that pretentiously repeated and even unspoken epithet(*diversity*)is that the East Bay populace supposedly consists of predominant percentages of asians, blacks and latinos!—as if those particular races alone exclusively made up the three sole ethnic "minorities" under the whole cosmic sun!

Yes, pretentious Bog-Bugs prudishly revel in performing their annual native American Indian Pow Wow for *"Indigenous Peoples Day"* in the place of celebrating *Columbus Day* like everybody else. But just how much more singularly, soundly and—*indigenously*—*RACIST* than that could you possibly get?

"People of color," perhaps? That's simply **colored people** with a preposition!

Incidentally, for those of you who put your misplaced trust in contrived, fabricated or otherwise manipulated statistics consult the so-called *"diversity index"* based on population figures for the year 2000 by the *US Census*: **Long Beach**, California ranked highest in "diversity"("different races or ethnicities"). **San Francisco** ranked lucky *13th* on the diversity index list. Face up to the truth, pretentious Bog-Bug babies: The Bog didn't even make the list—or the grade!

CHAPTER FOUR: CAFES, CREEPS & COLIC IN THE BOG

"The area's international population has encouraged a global range of cooking."—the City•*Stupid* guide

THE GOOD, THE BAD, THE FORGETTABLE: A CAFE ASSAY

Ah, Berserkeley—the Land of Garbage, Graffiti and Ecology(now if they'd only recycle the ankle-deep trash in the streets!)—all embodied in the cesspool city's politically correct but prideless coffee-contaminated cafe culture!

Is the cesspool city's cafe culture all the **RAGE**—or just an **OUTRAGE**? Can we tell the undiluted truth **WITHOUT WATERED-DOWN WHITEWASH** about its cafe corruption? **WHEREAS:**

•countless wanna-bes and would-bes turn into permanent fixtures sitting around pseudo-intellectualizing ad nauseum, ad infinitum about absolutely nothing of any sound substance.

•artsy-fartsy crowds down all manner of bitter, distasteful and unhealthy drinks to self-indulge their pretentions to European-hood.

•the coolest and hippest punks go to scam and be scammed.

•pampered and privileged Iranian political exiles go to hit on and pick up visiting au pair chicks.

•abysmal artwork(tossed out anyplace else!)adorning walls is on a par with quality toilet graffiti. "You are more likely to find local crafts than local arts," admits the City•*Stupid* guide. "And you're more likely to see them in coffeehouses and restaurants than in galler-

91

ies." And with good reason: no gallery worth its artless salt would exhibit that shit!

•so-called students—in a **MONUMENTAL** waste of time and talent—cram ad nauseum, ad infinitum to learn by rote and regurgitation all sorts of utterly worthless misinformation for collecting equally worthless diploma-mill degrees.

•coffee houses considered to be the haunts and hangouts of the cafe-crawling underground ought to be deeply buried precisely there: **underground!**

•profoundly misguided, self-professed, Christ-complexed saviors of the world set about grappling with the problems of the world—never quite grasping that their chosen cesspool of a "city" **IS** a frickin' problem of the world!!!

§

CRAPPY CAFES

If Cal(UC Berkeley)is the pseudo-intellectual hub of the backward, barbaric, butt-**UGLY** Bog of Berkeley then its crappy cafes and coffee houses are the focal points of contrary conversations—otherwise known as **BULLSHIT SESSIONS!**

Conversation in the Bog, puffs the City•*Stupid* guide, "is the number-one civic pastime, and right on its heels is food."

Cal students making what they strong-headedly believe to be academically or scholarly intellectual conversation show mostly that somehow, somewhere—likely by Cal's thought-passive puppet-ically correct indoctrination—they senselessly picked up the misguided notion that the childish compulsion to be pompously and pretentiously pseudo-intellectual by being irrationally and totally contrary to anything and everything amounts to thinking *"critically."* So they chronically confuse and misconceive the two to be synonymous. "It follows," puffs the *Insider's* guide, "that the kids are politically and globally aware." In a proverbial pig's eye! To them: to converse and discuss any subject or topic of controversy logically, rationally and reasoningly means only to **ARGUE** and **DEBATE** it relentlessly—and totally contrary to any and all logic, rationale or reason!

Sorry, punks, but no: childish contrariness for its own sake alone does not and never will equate with true *"critical thinking!"*

And the foremost meeting places to gather, rendezvous and pseudo-intellectualize at are of course the Bog's crappy cafes and coffee houses. So if you perversely enjoy and relish getting babbled at, harangued and harped on—as well as hit on since they're among the Bog's prime pickup places—then here's some select places to go(or avoid altogether):

Au Coquelet: there's one and one thing only that grudgingly recommends this dumpy and musty University Avenue cafe: its late-night closing hours—it's the only frickin' cafe in the Bog students can retreat to after all the others close. So after hours Bog-Bug cops go there too to get their stale donuts and muffins. Also it's where night-crawling gothic punks and "downtown" street people go. So be sure to wear your basic bland and tattered black to fit in with what the "good life" guide christens its "multi-faceted" clientele.

As far as atmosphere goes its brown-brick interior looks as utterly derelict as much of its clientele. Over its blaring sound system it plays the most god-*AWFUL* and overbearingly *OBNOXIOUS NOISE*(misnamed "music")ever to ring in your ears anywhere in the Bog. And the only more arrantly **ABYSMAL** "art" than that found and seen there hangs at an even more dismal Shattuck Avenue cafe called *Firenze*.

If this is supposed to be some sort of "underground" cafe its best bet would be to **BURY** itself as deep as **HELL** below underground **POSTHASTE!!!**

Its short-order staff used to loudly YELL at you at the top of their strained lungs to both call you to pick up your prepaid orders and again to throw you out of the dump at closing time before they finally resorted to customer service *numbers* and "reserved" dining signs—long since the student-ignored "no studying" signs flopped. After all, so long as you're there demeaning yourself by paying for its over-priced sandwiches, chips and salsa and rock gut wine you hardly deserve even to get any semblance of civil much less civilized customer service!

Cheapness *is* in fact this cafe's most distinguishing characteristic—witness its *chintzy* servings of sides(like french fries)and its equally *chintzy* "management" attitudes: its fanatic late-night lifer—flunky—vigilante will literally track you from room—to—room to make sure you don't "get away" with abusing your use of one of their paper cups! Just as its owner will actually accost you with some tired tirade about his "operating expenses" should he catch you taking a table for any number of minutes without ordering something! Strictly *lame-ass* and *low-class!*

Most entertaining hallmark: watching middle-aged regulars(as regular as plumbing fixtures!)surreptitiously stare at and **SCAM** pretty, young, stylish and studying coeds—most assuredly patiently waiting and biding their time until they can most gratefully finish doing whatever they have to do, **GET OUT** and go back to whatever preferred region they hailed from!

Berkeley Espresso. This smaller but airy, bright and mellower corner cafe at Shattuck and Hearest Avenues is supposedly(claims the "good life" guide)the prime place for patrons to revel in that arresting pastime of watching "the traffic go by as the cops write parking tickets at expired meters."

Cafe Milano: Supposedly *THE* student-fad cafe in the Bog it's at least where the greenest and most pubescent students go to over-crowd, slouch, scan, scam and—yes, sometimes—even study!

Its chief attraction: it's dirt-***CHEAP!***

And on most lukewarm days you can sit out at the open, sliding wall-windows facing the street, inhale and snuff up all that sweet-smelling sidewalk urine and auto exhaust fuming from the endlessly busy traffic clogging and congesting both your sinus passages as well as the nearby intersection of Bancroft Way and seamy and seedy Telegraph Avenue!

As for that frightfully ***BLEAK*** brick interior built from an alleyway of dark, drab concrete slabs, glass, iron and wood: if the Bog most assuredly looks like a nuclear wasteland—and it does!—then this cafe most assuredly resembles its most desolate and despairing looking ***BOMB SHELTER!***

If you go there you've really gone and hit ***ROCK BOTTOM:*** so just bend over, put your head between your knobby knees and kiss your annihilated ass ***GOOD BYE!!!***

Caffe Strada: Now this is the Bog's most honest-to-goodness mass production and assembly line cafe complete with classical music piped in from a local public broadcasting radio station. All it's missing of course is the ubiquitous people-moving conveyer belt rolling robotic customers in and out, to and from the service counter!

"Next person in line!" is the indifferently shouted and care-*LESS* greeting you'll typically be met with on stepping up to the counter. Each and every time I hear that cattle call I feel like looking all around myself and asking the counter clerk: *"Why don't you help the next biped mollusk in line first?"*

This is also often the most overcrowded cafe—who in hell knows why?!—where prospective patrons circle all around, hovering over benches, booths and tables like swooping vultures in search of rotting and decaying animal carcasses! So charming!

Beware as well of those spry dive-bombing sparrows who'll strafe your outdoor table with putrid and sappy bird-droppings!

Recommended though are its scrumptious ham–and–cheese croissants—when they're stocked, which is rare.

Speaking of rotting and reeking things this cafe boasts proudly of having the out–and–out **SCUZZIEST** and most **DISGUSTING** toilet in all the Bog—where more often than not you'll be standing and sloshing shit-deep in overflowed toilet water and turds! And its graffiti-plastered walls offer the lowest of incoherent and illiterate low-life gibberish!

Finally, this is the most creep-infested cafe to plague the Bog. Overrun during the summer by rowdy and rambunctious high-schoolers without a life the next largest cafe contingent of pests to so persistently plague the place are horny, on–the–prowl Middle Eastern types(translate: money-pampered, privileged, hair-greased, cologne-reeking, gold chain-sporting, *BMW*-driving Iranian or Iraqi political exiles)on the hot scent of young and fresh, lone, liberated and loose au pair girls from faraway lands in search of foreign adventure, intrigue and romance—in Berkeley?!—but getting, instead, a whole lot of disappointing and disillusioning one-night stands(if that!)!

Most amusing—or mawkish—hallmark, depending on your point of view: watching the hilarious antics and escapades of these desperately on–the–make Middle Easterners, thinking quite self-deludedly they're the last of the great lovers left stalking the face of the earth!

Repeated like clockwork twice daily at the cafe's two separate social hours—6:30pm and 9:30pm—their monotonously basic drill for the prowl plays out more or less like this:

•Once they get their typically one–and–only bottomless beverage at the service counter inside they go to the condiment counter to stand and look out the cafe's front windows so they can survey the benches and tables outside for those lone au pair girls—all the while mindlessly stirring, sloshing and spilling their lone drink all over the countertop!

•Failing that for spotting any prospective pickups they then slowly slink and skulk all around among the benches and tables outside—mindless beverage in hand—looking all around, reconnoitering for women who are supposed to notice them but seldom do!

•And failing that they gather together—mindless beverages in hand—standing in a circle in the middle of the cafe entryway, making a grand display and showy spectacle of themselves, pretending to boisterously talk together, strutting, swaggering but all the while looking all around in the vain, false and forlorn hope that the cafe's women are looking back and rabidly lusting after all of them! As Ripley would say incredulously: *"Believe it, or not!"*

•Most fun and funny antic: watching one of them

stupidly hit on some bitchy California chick and getting told quite bluntly to: *"Fuck off!"*

Some people never change their act but these gnarly guys are growing **OLD** and **GREY** rehashing theirs!

Capoeria. This City•*Stupid* guide-designated "coffee shop and performance space" on Addison Street most consistently hires some of the haughtiest(and hairiest!)and most uppity counter service chicks in all the Bog. And its light-weight, underdeveloped "Latin" groupies honestly but misguidedly really do think that they're bodybuilders and that their wussy capoeria dance really is an effective street martial art!

Espresso Roma: At the corner of College and Ashby Avenues this cafe is spacious, spongy and grungy—and if done up right could very well be your stereotypically *"Beat"* cafe. But, alas, at night it's just your stereotypically lively student study–and–pickup place!

Though somewhat distant from the "downtown" Bog it's conveniently located right next door to the *Elmwood Theater* as a logical stopping-off point to relax and take a bite, a drop or a piss on your way to see the movies!

About those supposedly "art"-adorned walls you needn't even go there.

Among gossip-mongers, though, this cafe is rumored to have been the original *Cafe Roma* located in times past at the present site of the now *Cafe Strada*(at the corner of Bancroft Way and College Avenue)—before greedy landlords refused to renew the *Roma* owners' property lease so they themselves could cash in on the overwhelming financial success the original *Cafe Roma* owners had made of the booming business now known as *Cafe Strada!*

Now that's the anti-chain, anti-gentrification *Berkeley* way! *Espresso Roma* also reportedly operates the

I-House Cafe.

International House Cafe(with its "glassed-in area," over-exaggerates the *Insider's* guide, "that looks down Bancroft Way to San Francisco Bay."). Now this is just too, **TOO FRICKIN' MUCH!** It's the type of hype that makes you really wonder whether people actually do **GO** to see and be at the places they **BLUFF, HUFF** and **PUFF** about!

But if you can sit at the *I-House Cafe*(perched high up atop steep Bancroft Way)sipping anything, much less a "giant cappuccino" as the "good life" guide gloats, and still "enjoy the view of the Golden Gate Bridge" spanning San Francisco and Marin's foothills—even on the clearest of "clear" days—then all I've gotta say is: lend me your frickin' **TELESCOPE!!!**

Mediterraneum Caffe. This is that venerated timeworn hot-spot where die-hard if aging, graying, passe, pony-tailed hippies still go to hang out and—as the City•*Stupid* guide so aptly puts it—"rail" at "The Man," "The Establishment" and "The System." Today, though, the "good life" guide claims that it's "somewhat less an anti-bourgeois magnet" than in its anarchist heyday.

Nefeli Caffe: Owned and run with the stylish flair and panache by the very same two cultivated Greek partners who used to run their now-defunct *Odyssia* bistro—*Naso and Pascal*—this warmly romantic little cafe north of Cal campus at Euclid and Hearst Avenues brings the sole fresh and refreshing authentic breath of Mediterranean air(not to mention purely brewed coffee and impeccably prepared salads and sandwiches) ever to breeze through the severely stifling and suffocating Bog!

Of all the most virtuous traits propelling this particular excellent and exemplary exception of a commendable cafe before, ahead and beyond all other cafes in the Bog is the single most significant quality that all the rest fail and fall far short of ever coming even close to displaying: **CONTINENTAL CHARM AND CLASS!**

Complimentary praise alone could scarcely pay worthy tribute to the perfection this "little lady" of a cafe sets its consistently artistic seal to—from its musically cosmopolitan atmosphere to its thoroughly friendly, hard-working, helpful and service-minded staff!

"Service is pretentious and slow," whined the "good life" guide.

Well, bitter Bog-Bugs calling its gracious, personalzied and polished service "pompous," preferring to be called like cattle rather than being greeted and treated like decent, dignified and respectable human beings deserve to **SWIM** gleefully in the sloshing slop and sludge of *Strada!*

RE-JECTS:

Pretentious Peet's, Royal Ground, Starbucks and Tully's

"**I**f you want to gather an angry crowd in Berkeley," cants the City•*Stupid* guide, "just announce that you're putting a Starbucks in their neighborhood."

Well, the Bog now has some *four Starbucks* coffee houses to its incursive corporate credit so its ineffectual "angry" crowds appear to be pretty inept at stemming the height much less the tide of their own phoniness and pretention!

I hate to break it to you, bitter Bog-Bug babies, but the actual decaffeinated scoop of the matter is this: local darling, pet "home-brewed favorite"—*Peet's*—in actual point of fact **SPAWNED** *Starbucks!!!*

One of three *Starbucks* co-founders, Jerry Baldwin trained under his Dutch immigrant mentor and *Peet's* owner, Alfred Peet, before starting the Seattle-based *Starbucks*. Ultimately Baldwin *sold* out his interest in *Starbucks* only to return to the Bog to *buy* out *Peet's* *sell*-out of his own coffee company.

It's home-brewed coffee quackery that could only be

home-grown in the phony and pretentious Bog!

Those whining, anti-gentrificationist, bitter Bog-Bug crybabies criticizing and carping at the clean, comfortable and brightly lit if over-refrigerated study hall-friendly "chain" cafes(*Royal Ground*, *Starbucks* and *Tully's*)simply can't be happy or pleased unless their feet slosh in the swirling shit and toilet water overflowing the rest room floor—just like at stupendous *Strada!* They'd much rather lap up all that acrid and acerbic slop and sludge served up at most other Bog cafes—*Strada's* **specialty!**

WATCH OUT, then, bitter Bog-Bug babies! Gentrified, shopping-mall suburbia may just be right around the corner, creeping up to overtake and overrun all the Bog quicker than you might think: after all, several exceptionally pleasant and cheerful such "chain" coffee houses—some complete with richly furnished, salon-style sitting room parlors—have already opened up to booming business in the Bog!

VIVA Gentrification! **VIVA** Suburbia! **VIVA** Berkeley **BASHING!**

If tie–dyed–in–the–wool Berkeleyite anarchists ever had their druthers their revolutionary rallying cry would be triggering a bowel movement for: **GHETTO–fication!!!!**

BITS OF THE BOG: COCKEYED COFFEE

Aw, poor, overworked, cry-***BABIES!*** It's such an imposition and inconvenience—such a curse to coffee culture, some absurdly insist—to actually ask the coffee house counter *flunky* to describe the different and distorted kinds of coffee in existence!

Oh no! Geez, for pity's sake, don't you dare put yourself out for a customer about to pay an hour or more of your minimum slave-wage! That would be utterly unthinkable! You just might *pull* something—like a vocal cord!

You know, what's really amusing about all these pompous and snobbish coffee freaks, misguidedly thinking it's so chic and cool to torturously sip and pretend to relish swallowing all that bitter-tasting, muddy and unhealthy coffee swill—*Cafe Au Lait, Caffe Espresso, Caffe Latte, Caffe Mocha, Cappuccino*...blah, blah, ***BLAH!***—is how much alike they resemble their prohibited *smoking* cohorts as they witlessly cut short their natural life spans by unnumbered years!

Yeah, they're oh-***SO*** *cool!*

Well, drink yourself into an early, premature death as you please! Just don't try to convert me to your half-witted stupidity—accosting me while I'm training at the gym, trying to sell me your lousy unsolicited advice that caffeine will somehow miraculously energize, stimulate and intensify my workouts. True fact of the matter is: coffee excites hyperactive anxiety and tension—not to mention dehydration—more than anything else!

So save it for the superstitious!

CAFETERIA COLIC

O akland and the Bog, eulogizes the *Insider's guide*, "are also centers of ethnic cuisine." ***Really?*** Who the frick do they really think they're frickin' kidding???!!!

When it really comes to all those "ethnic" restaurants, so-called, supposedly ***SO*** ample and abundant all over the frickin' backward, barbaric, butt-***UGLY*** Bog of Berkeley the most asinine and inane euphemism, the most idiotic and imbecilic misnomer bandied all about so absurdly, so laughably, so ludicrously, so ridiculously, so ***STUPIDLY*** is that overused, misused and ultra-abused word: ***AUTHENTIC!***

Now what the frick does this mean and in what frickin' sense? That the food itself is authentic—or just the restaurant? That the food's ingredients are authentic? That the cooks or chefs—or the table-servers—are authentic? That the way they cook, prepare or serve the food is authentic? What, what, ***WHAT???***

What it invariably and most typically means in the Bog is strictly this: the food of one "ethnic" group—whether *authentically* cooked, prepared and served or not—is in fact and in reality cooked, prepared and served by yet another, entirely different "ethnic" group typically to suit and satisfy *American* taste!

So can the bitter Bog ever get real and ever get over itself long enough to ever admit the total truth of its ethnically culinary pretentiousness?!

Let's see, shall we? Here then is just a small sampling of the Bog's more colic-causing "ethnic" eateries:

Arinell Pizza. Yeah, it may be just a closet—even gamy—joint in the "downtown" Bog but it's absolutely the only joint in the whole wide Bog that serves a perfectly bitchin', nasty but *non*-travesty slice of pizza!

Sorely missed though is the now-defunct ***Pirro's***. Painted on its storefront window on south Shattuck Avenue used to be a prohibition sign crossing out in red *"pretentious dining!"* **YEAH, BABY, YEAH!!!**

The *"good life"* guide condemned its food as "predictable" with "not much bang for the buck."

But in distant times past its T-shirt-attired staff served up to perfection their positively peerless pizza—unsurpassed anyplace else in the entire frickin' Bog before or since!

Not only "bang for the buck" but the **BIGGEST** and **BEST BANG**—precisely because of the glutting, over-abundant **OVERKILL** of abysmally piss-poor and pretentious pizza places all over the frickin' Bog!

Blessedly ***Arinell's*** isn't amongst them!

Bette's Oceanview Diner. Supposedly a classic, dinky(if shiny)50s-style diner serving all-American fare on 4th Street near the marina in the west Bog with arduous weekend waits for seating of up to a full hour or more there's no view of San Francisco Bay much less the ocean! Pretentious Bog-Bugs wait out that hour or more with truth for a marvelous view of dilapidated buildings and run-down railroad tracks!("Oh," apologizes the "good life" guide, "by the way there is no view of the ocean so don't get your hopes up for it."). "On Sunday mornings," puffs the City•*Stupid* guide, "young, arty academic couples who've just spent the night together line up to wait an hour or more for breakfast at this small, shiny diner, a Berkeley institution since 1982." Unless he's some sort of pervert spending most of his Saturday nights out voyeuring all around all over the

Bog how the guide's hack happens to know who spends their nights with whom much less who's amongst the most arty-farty in the Bog is still something of an esoteric mystery!

Rick and Ann's, close to the Claremont Hotel, "has quaint written all over it"—or so gloats the *"good life"* guide—and is where the City•*Stupid* guide claims "breakfast is king."(in the Bog that translates to *boorish* not to mention *boring!*).

And like **Bette's "Oceanview" Diner** it's supposed to have "crowds queuing up" on weekends for brunch waits of an hour or more! But if you've **EVER** even **ENTERTAINED** the ever so silly and stupid notion of waiting for up to a full frickin' hour or more just to gain entrance to any hash house in the Bog then I feel powerfully sorry for you: you've got to be one of the dumbest of duped and defrauded dopes alive!!!

Overmuch is made of the fact that it's "run by a husband and wife team." Well, so is the snug and cozy closet space on University Avenue called the **Makris Cafe**—only its marital "team" is Korean and its conspicuously cooked(out in the open and in full view)countertop breakfast is simply homespun and superior in every last respect!

Mournfully missed is the **UC Cafe**—most affectionately also known simply as *"The Uk!"*—the coziest and homiest sit–down–booth–joint on University Avenue to eat Sunday brunch at until, that is, its family owners sold out to an inelegant annex of **Nation's** *Hamburgers*.

Even more mournfully missed is the late but long-extinct **Edy's** restaurant on Shattuck Avenue whose space is now occupied by *Eddie Bauer Inc.*

Blondie's Pizza. Ah, yes, the absolute perfect place to sit at window-less, open-air front counters and get picked off as a stationary target in a drive-by shooting on Telegraph Avenue!

It's no wonder this grimy, slimy little dump–in–the–wall would come to "symbolize" getting gastritis in the Bog—what with its thick slabs of gelatinous *soy* product(no, it's *not* cheese!)plastered like mortar onto even thicker slices of cardboard-like crust and deceptively called pizza!

No doubt you could lay bricks with the stuff! So how could your poor tortured stomach do anything else *but* turn???

Blue Nile. Now I literally **LOVE** this: the Ethiopian food served here is supposed to be "authentic" simply because you have to scoop it up with bread and eat it with your fingers! Which may of course very well be but the restaurant feeding you that line most certainly saves on its cost of eating utensils!

"Forget about forks and spoons," gloats the City•*Stupid* guide. Hell, if that's all it takes to be "authentic": stay home, throw out the silverware and eat your *Starkist* tuna straight from the can!

Bongo Burger. After being stuck fast in the Bog for nearly two frickin' decades I still can't help but wonder whether the Iranian exiles who christened this little chintzy charbroiler chain didn't *really* mean **BONZO!!!** They're *super*-chintzy with their fries too!!!!

Brennan's. Founded by its namesake brothers even before *Spenger's* in 1878 as a livery and saloon it morphed in 1959 into what the *"good life"* guide dubs a "down-home, all-American restaurant" catering strictly(and cheaply)to the Bog's "eclectic" but strapped meat–and–potatoes set!

Buttercup. Read whatever subliminal message you like into this but once I dated briefly the cutest if most delectably corpulent young black chick who used to waitress at this "country-style" College Avenue eatery and: she used to crossly call it the *"ButterFUCK!"*

Cafe De La Paz. This is one of the few truly authentic and superior ethnic restaurants located in the north Bog's gourmet–and–gastritis ghetto for eating the most incredibly flavorful Latin American food—where you can actually watch from your table your "authentic" Latin American cooks preparing your food through the aquarium glass window of their kitchen!

What this place really needs to do to perfect its otherwise perfect atmosphere is: hire some truly authentic Latina Americana table-servers and get rid of those curt California chicks from the north Bog burbs!

It's neither "eclectic" nor "unusual" with lots of "potential" as the *"good life"* guide grudgingly equivocates: it's merely **REAL!** Go there!

Cafe Durant. Supposedly people go up, up and away to this rooftop cafe misguidedly thinking they'll somehow rise above and escape all the clamorous noise and smutty pollution lying low on the Bog's seamy and seedy streets far off below—as *if* all the obnoxious racket and just plain noxious stench of the Bog couldn't and didn't waft up to and beyond even the highest and loftiest of mountain tops much less ramshackle rooftops! *Wrong!*

Cafe Intermezzo. Here that tired old stand-by for bad food(made absolutely no better by humongous servings of grass in big wooden bowls!)and surly service is in full force: watching with pretentious fascination while you eat the supposedly trendy and *"diverse crowd!"*

"Whatever happened to sprouts?" exults the City•*Stupid* guide. Well, I'll tell you: this place serves huge haystacks of sprouts as filler stuff to cover its paucity of other portions! For that matter then whatever happened to eating like a frickin' **_GOAT???!!!_**

So come up with another, better rabbit's alibi or excuse for eatin' *that* shit up!

Cha-Am and Plearn Thai Cuisine. Forget all the hyperbolical **_HYPE_** put out about either of these two Thai places!

Suffice it to say, all over-publicized puffery aside: huddling human herds answering the very same cattle call and led far astray by the very same misguiding, misinforming and misleading publicity may very well flock sheepishly(in "throngs" gloats the *"good life"* guide!)to the very same fad restaurants—but that hardly makes the food served either more or less than mediocre if not outright inferior!

Superior by far in both quality and quantity is **Dara Thai/Lao Cuisine**, nestled atop the very same steep perch in the big, beautiful old house right next door to *Cha-Am*, or even the more modest and humble but comfortably cozy **Thai Delight Cuisine** nestled below a block away on Shattuck Avenue in the gourmet–and–gastritis ghetto of the north Bog.

Chester's Cafe. Now here I must openly confess: on one of those richly rare lukewarm and somewhat sunny spring days on an early Sunday afternoon in the Bog, following an especially full night of wallowing passionately in sheer, sumptuous lovemaking—atop the wooden, open-air sun deck upstairs in the north Bog's pleasant *Walnut Square* is the ideally perfect place to share a delicious eggs Benedict brunch, English muffins and orange juice with your sweet and sensuous lover! All that's missing is a warm and breezy ocean-bound beach! But at least from that elevated deck—unlike pretentious *Bette's Oceanview Diner*—you can actually see(and view)even if at quite a distance the San Francisco Bay!

One and only one place comparable for paying the very same pleasurable visit was the now-defunct **Continental Garden Restaurant** on south Shattuck Avenue(replaced by the surprisingly stylish "French" restaurant named **La Note**)which boasted the Bog's most beautiful, private and intimate open-air garden booths and proudly served up the Bog's tastiest and most heavenly hollandaise sauce!

Its much mourned passing is deeply sad and sorrowful.

Chez Panisse. Yes, little else can be said with wasted words over-praising this ultimate and elite model of a scandalously over-rated and over-publicized fad restaurant(and "mecca of California cuisine," gushes the *"good life"* guide)all right!

"This is certainly the East Bay's," likewise gushes the *Insider's* guide, "and some would say the whole country's, most famous restaurant."

Yeah, right! But if getting royally roped in to pay excessively exorbitant prices for the skimpiest and most paltry portions of the blandest and most **BORING** frickin' food imaginable is the stupidest and most witless thing you could ever be into then by all means: this is **THE** paragon of a place to stupidly fritter away not only all the last vestiges of your human pride, dignity and self-respect but also all the money you can muster, mister!

And no—not even some other chump paying the over-ostentatiously extravagant tab makes **NONE** of it any more palatable!

"The style of cooking is restrained;" equivocates the *Insider's* guide. "some people call it 'Shaker California,' or 'Zen California'..."

Yeah, well, I call it **SHAKE-DOWN** *California cuisine!* And its founding shyster, Alice Waters, should re-christen herself Alice **Watered**-*Down* because that's just what both her dishes and menus are—though the tabs most assuredly aren't!

She's a crafty charlatan though: she set up a slightly cheaper upstairs a la carte *"cafe"* serving up the same slop to make its pinched patrons *think* they're getting an organic bargain while making her more opulent patrons downstairs *think* they're getting something superior for *famine* prices! **Famine** in fact describes more accurately and truthfully the food than the prices at this price–and–purse–gouging establishment!

Pure pretense and pretension in the Bog in the **EXTREME!** So does that just about soundly sum things up? Enough said, finally!

Except that: Alice *Watered-Down* fomented not so much a food *"revolution"* as a regurgitating food **REVERSION!**

In May 2001 Alice *Watered-Down* told *Biography* magazine she liked eating food *"that's alive."* Beware of being served that extraordinary entree that starts to sluggishly crawl off your plate before you've even had a chance to stick it with your fork!

Orville Schell, dean of the UC Berkeley graduate school of journalism, has luridly likened her restaurant to a "little liberated zone in the midst of a huge occupied territory."

Chez Panisse is a little money-siphoning pit sunk smack dab in the middle of an even more immense and mammoth pit—the backward, barbaric, butt-**UGLY** Bog!

Claremont Diner. Forget the burlesque *Bette's* blatant parody of a diner—even one with a reputed but nonexistent *"Oceanview!"*

Classic is the word most perfectly and truly synonymous with an uncorrupted and incorruptible diner experience like you'll relish at the black–and–white tiled **Claremont** Avenue diner—no relation whatever except by moniker to that pretentious *Claremont Resort* at the Bog-Oakland border—which even tiny ads run in the Bog's local ad-glutted weekly, the *Express*(more aptly re-named the *Excess*)can't spoil or taint!

Its two–for—one weekly dinner coupons for the heartiest of classic diner fare simply can't be beat anywhere else in the entire frickin' Bog!

And its comfortable, high-backed, red-leather booths are private and intimate: there you can sumptuously suck both shake straws and generously giving tongues with equal and reckless abandon!

Downtown. "Berkeley," bluffs, huffs and puffs the *Insider's* guide, "has experienced a downtown renaissance, with...this sensational new restaurant...appropriately named..."

Well, that eternal question yet forever remains: *WHAT* frickin' **"*DOWNTOWN*"???!!!** There *is* no frickin' *"downtown"* in all the Bog!!! And if you honestly and truly believe that the Bog embodies the site of some imaginary "renaissance" then it's really high time that you got the hell outta Dodge and headed for Florence, Italy!

This extremely pretentious and supposedly "stylish" Shattuck Avenue eatery aspires(but ultimately flops)to rout nearby *Le Theatre*(formerly *Gertie's Chesapeake Bay*)for its undue fair share of the *Berkeley Repertory Theatre* groupie crowd with reputed "entertainment"—inferior and mediocre amateur "Live jazz and blues" bands which are about as insipid and vapid as this bland dump's food!

Then there's that reputedly *chatty* "wait staff"—the most telling tip-off of all to its rank amateurism!

There's hardly anything more frickin' irritating than

"chatty" table-servers persistently intruding as obnoxiously and offensively as they possibly can on both your peace and privacy—as if you came to the frickin' joint just so they could obtrusively invite themselves to dine along with you and royally screw up your entire dining experience and enjoyment!

Like, just plunk down the spread and get *lost,* ***PUNK FLUNKY!***

Encore Hot Pot City(now defunct). How would you like to go to a restaurant for an *indoor* backyard barbeque?

Well, that's essentially what you sumptuously enjoy at this one–cheap–price–pays–all–you–can–cook–yourself–and–eat barbeque buffet on University Avenue where it's all too easy to voraciously over-gorge yourself and over-indulge even your heartiest appetite! So go hungry!

Once inside its sparkling, brightly shining interior you feel utterly jubilant and exhilarated as at your leisurely pleasure you freely pick and choose from among ***ALL KINDS*** of fresh meat, seafood and vegetables either to boil or grill to eat at your very own private hot pot–and–barbeque cookery table!

Of course rice, condiments, desserts and drinks go right along with *Encore's* new and novel Chinese ***FEAST***—one of the most savory eateries you could ever, ***EVER*** savor or even ***HOPE*** to savor in the Bog! Service is sterling! And the bus men are as friendly as they are spiritedly proficient!

Fatapple's Restaurant and Bakery. Another fad *fast* food joint in the north residential Bog. "The worst part about Fatapple's," boasts the *"good life"* guide, "is deciding what to get..."

Once you get past the tediously persistent hype about its bakery and brunch you'll find out that the "worst part" about the place is that it serves no real frickin' **DINNERS**(unless burgers and deli-style sandwiches are your idea of dinners)even though it deceptively pretends to offer "dinner platters"—or at least a dinner *time!*

Why bitter Bog-Bugs line up outside waiting to gain entrance to this dumpy place is way beyond me—especially since there's no space to wait inside and a condescending sign admonishes waiting patrons to stand behind its barn-door gate until seated.

Don't be done-*IN* by its dinner-*LESS* menu and don't say I didn't warn you!

Fat Slice Pizza. Supposedly the "chief competition of *Blondie's*..." there is no frickin' competition—*Fat Slice's* pizza is far better and far superior to *Blondie's* by frickin' interstellar light-years(think the original *Star Trek* TV theme!)! At least their pizza has some tasty tomato sauce to go along with the cheese-glob and, unlike *Blondie's*, the cheese–to–crust ratio is much more proportionate.

Behind the chunk–o–crust you get at *Blondie's* their motto about cheese and sauce must be: *a little dab'll do 'ya!*

Fenton's. Forget about wasting your time paying even one wasted visit to wait outside in the frickin' cold in incredibly overlong lines(what the frickin' attraction is I've yet to frickin' figure out!)to set stupid foot into this drab, dreary, dull and dilapidated ice–creamery–eatery in Oakland—even for its poopy ice cream! Perfectly depressing!

I mention it purely in passing—and in memory of its richly comfortable and cozy little offshoot once keeping shop in the snug niche in the north Bog on Euclid Avenue now occupied by *Nefeli Cafe*: **SKYLER'S!**

Lined with shelves crammed with books and soft-cushioned seats, looking and feeling more like a small book shop than an ice cream shop, *Skyler's* used to be the most heavenly and ideal spot to pause for coffee, a scrumptious hot fudge sundae and a very good read!

Like the *Continental Garden Restaurant, Skyler's* is a place mournfully missed!

Flint's Bar-B-Q. Yeah, yeah, yeah: more people lining up and waitin' in line for, well, not a whole frickin' lot really!

Small is its shack!

Saucy is its stack!

Puppet-ically correct 'cause it's black!

Could we be settin' dat to rap???

Supposedly serving up some of the Bog's best barbeque it's heavier on the 'Q 'cause they do heap and pile it on pretty thick—*gobs* of it, *TONS* of it!

But my perennial question is: where's the frickin' *BEEF???!!!* Or for that matter the *pork(or chicken)?!*

This place makes time profitably by serving up some of the most meat-*LESS*(as in sauce-spread bones!)barbeque around! Agin, you bin duly warned!

Hey! How's my *Ebonics?*

Gertie's Chesapeake Bay Cafe(now Le Theatre). Unless you're just stupid–is–as–stupid–does this place is *NOT* "hard to find"(as the *"good life"* guide so stupidly contends)simply because it's nestled snug in the middle of a building's cloistered "court" off and in-between either Addison Street or University Avenue! I mean, how *can* you miss that *pansy PINK* decor or those lighted menus stuck fast to the outside walls on either end of the court alleyway???!!!

And its seafood dishes *are* somewhat savory.

What *is* difficult and distressing to deal with, quite precisely, is the primly proper, pompous and conspicuously pretentious *Berkeley Rep* theatre groupies who too typically haunt the place! Beware!

Giovanni's and Venezia. You can most handily and justifiably lump together these two long-time, supposedly *"Italian"* fad restaurants perniciously persisting in the Bog—for neither are they authentic nor even *insipidly* Italian!

Yes, I am mostly Italian, thank you—and I can tell you quite unequivocally and unabashedly: none of the food dished up at either of these places remotely approaches being even *illusorily* Italian!

"The pastas are well done, too," the City•*Stupid* guide equivocates about *Venezia*, "because they're not weighted down by heavy sauces." Translation: the sauces are mightily **WATERED** down!

In fact, I wouldn't even be at all surprised if lying hidden in the deepest and nethermost freezer vaults of both dumps to be broken open and laid bare were over-sized, jumbo jars of wholesale supermarket spaghetti sauce bearing those spine-chillingly ominous and forbidding commercial labels: **Prego** and **Ragu!!**

Yes, that's just how bad, sad and outright piss-poor these places actually are!

At *Giovanni's* on south Shattuck Avenue tables are crammed close together to make the most of its confined, cramped and crowded space(despite a misnamed "Boat Room")to prompt at the same time both the greatest attendance and the greatest attrition since there's no opportunity for romantic patrons to relish either their privacy or intimacy—much less **Amore**, *Italian* Style!

Over-much is made of that "real-life laundry line" strung out across one corner of the room at *Venezia* on University Avenue—as if prospective patrons were just *dying to dine underneath somebody's dirty drawers!*

Try instead **Fontina Caffe Italiano** on Shattuck

Avenue in the north Bog—it's still *un*-authentic Middle Eastern-Italian but there at least they manage to conjure up a far more credible *illusion* of Italiana!

Salerno at the opposite end of the Avenue in the south Bog *finally folded* after untold years of perfecting that newfangled but very unsavory concoction: *Mexican*-Italian cuisine!!!

If you ever dared risking your stomach's safety to find out what *that* meant by means of *turning* your stomach then by all means you deserved getting the runs!

Homemade Cafe. At this runty restaurant on Sacramento Street in the west Bog run by rude and even runtier staff the petty emphasis is on rapid turn-over! So forget about relishing any semblance of a cozy and romantic "sunny" Sunday brunch–in–a–private–booth with your dearest, dearly beloved: if you overlooked their condescending booth-quota sign at the entrance their booth *Gestapo* will just threaten to seat and cram the next party of *five* strangers right alongside you! Outright obnoxious!

Jupiter. No doubt you'd have a passel more fun on the actual planet(if only you could take a local *Khalsa* taxicab to get there!)than at this over-glorified beer bar!

And if the crowd's as "mellow" as the *"good life"* guide crowingly claims then they're likely more maudlin than merry—no doubt because it's staffed excessively with what I call **peon punks with attitudes**: puerile *flunkys* whose pert demeanor far exceeds their lowly station in low-life!

Oh yeah, real winners all!

So when they do get uppity with you just ask them just how much an hour *do* they get paid to mop up the vomit barfed up by cheap drunks puking from listening to lame-ass jazz in their enchanting "beer garden"—suitably situated behind the dingy brown brick building which the *Insider's* guide fantasizes "looks more like Snow White's castle than a brewpub."

If that's the case then it's the perfect place for patrons dubbed **Dumpy** to patronize!

Head instead for comfy and cushiony **Spats** farther north on Shattuck Avenue to devour a delectable teriyaki chicken sandwich along with your choice cocktail!

La Cascada. Once upon a time in the Bog there was *La Burrita, La Fiesta, El Sombrero, Cancun* and yes, even *Bingo Burrito*—in fact, they're still there, barely—but then there came *La Cascada*(the waterfall!)on sometimes sunny Center Street near *Starbucks* at the very foot of Cal's cross-campus road!

It's the very same thing that separates *Burger King* from *MacDonald's,* propelling one far ahead to beat out all the others in high-quality to rise and reach an impeccable and incomparable league all their own—the success- and supremacy-making ingredient being: meat charbroiled over a flaming grill rather than fried over a hot-metal stovetop!

So broiling and grilling over frying is the best burrito's very simple secret really!

All the rest, your honor—including the spicy-hot condiments—is superfluously incompetent, irrelevant and immaterial!

Zona Rosa, we miss you: you used to be the best before you so tragically left us!!! **Fabuloso** must've been pretty fantastical, though, since it temporarily took over your spot before being displaced itself!

La Val's. WHATEVER you do **DO NOT EAT** this **NASTY** dump's **NAUSEATING** onion-infested lasagna, so-called: not a whole lot worse than its disgusting pizza—it looks like vomit, it tastes like vomit, it will **MAKE** you vomit!!!

"Try the food," barfs the "good life" guide, "you'll be back. Warning, this may be addictive." Since when did retching vomit ever get to be addictive???!!!

Le Bateau Ivre. This is one of those rarest of Bog gems and precious jewels combining both classic charm and all-out blood-warming, breath-panting, breath-taking, cheek-blushing, chest-heaving, eye-pleasing, flesh-flushing, heart-stopping, heart-throbbing, mouth-quivering, palm-sweating, pulse-pumping, skin-sooth-ing, toe-tingling and vital-burning **PASSION** and **ROMANCE**—to say nothing of the tastiest strawberry milk shake to be relished and savored anyplace else in the entire heartless and passionless Bog!

That's why it's so hard to believe its French name translates to the *Drunken Boat!*

Take no notice of that: but go there only with some-one very, very special—and you'll remain rightfully oblivious to even the ever so vile "view," so-called, of ramshackle south Telegraph Avenue rotting right be-fore your eyes right outside your window!

Yep, the drunken boat put the pretentious and over-priced Shattuck Avenue *Metropole* to pathetic, pitiful shame—not to mention right out of business!

Mandarin Garden. Once you pass through the front door, even before you set foot into the dimly but warmly lit interior of gilded red and gold and the some-what melancholy but melodic and mellowing music falls on your unsuspecting ears, you step beneath softly tin-kling wind chimes and pass by a gently trickling rock garden and wishing well—you realize right away that you've been immediately immersed in an exquisitely el-egant and enchanting Chinese wonderland, surround-ed by a soothing and tranquil atmosphere full of the sweetly sensual sights, sounds and of course scents of the mysterious and mystical Orient!

Here's the absolute best of the best Chinese restaurants in the Bog whose act none can follow where you're entranced and transported to utter joy and delight in both spirit as well as taste!

"The menu, however," pompously grumbles the *"good life"* guide, "could be updated to appeal to sophisticated Bay Area palates. Most frequenters of local Chinese restaurants no longer need to be offered dishes 'a la Hunan' or 'a la Szechuan.' But for this reason, Mandarin Garden could be a good place to take older visiting relatives for Chinese food."

While the others may try to lure and beguile you with props and backdrops backed up by flavorless food this paradisiacal restaurant is for younger and older alike the real deal—and it most definitely needs no updating to appease the pompous and pretentious "Bay Area palates!"

King Dong, further south on Shattuck Avenue with no uncouth relations to kingly schlongs, runs a close second with its perfectly pleasant atmosphere and impeccably prepared and served food.

Taiwan Restaurant on University Avenue runs a close third only because it's cheaper—not tastier—it's wanting in atmosphere and it readily reverts to the overactive rather than relaxed assembly line–and–mass–production–style of service!

Berkeley Sun Hong Kong. This pre-prepared, *really*-fast(Chinese)food place runs the distant fourth and merits most honorable mention if only because it's the only place in the whole frickin' Bog that stays open(until 2am)for night-prowling owls later on weeknights than the "underground"–aspiring–and–undeserving *Au Coquelet Cafe!* And the white shirt–with–black jacket–attired wait staff doesn't even shout at you at the top of their strained lungs to throw you out at closing time!

At once bitter and tasty their *won ton noodles soup* is erratically appetizing. More consistently tantalizing, though, are their *prawns&vegetable chow mein* over *crispy noodles* and *sliced fish mixed with cream corn on rice* dishes—all incredibly cheap at the price!

Yangtze River Restaurant. In spite of its ritzy green, red and yellow tiled archway, token courtyard and voluminous fish tank at its entrance and its helpful and hospitable wait staff—or even its prime location in the gastritis–and–gourmet ghetto on Shattuck Avenue in the north Bog—this sadly disappointing place simply fails to deliver the goods—or for that matter the good food!

Long Life Vegi House. Sorry, but this overrated joint on University Avenue suffers from the worst and most severe case of the *3Ps*: pitiful food, paltry portions and pathetic service! The same goes for that *Long Life Noodle Company and Jook Joint* too—in spite of its spiffy facade.

Oscar's. Forget *Barney's* or *Mel's the Original* sorry chain-fried excuses for burgers—*Oscar's* is as greasy, grimy and grungy a dive as it should be but it's *charbroiled* burgers and deep-fried fries are wholly *genuine!*

"It's hard to believe," marvels the *"good life"* guide, "that Oscar's has never been razed or renovated, especially on a street with high property values like Shattuck."

How does this grease-glazed dive survive and avoid being leveled and razed from among all the other first-class and high-class(translate: last-class and low-class)greasy spoons on Shattuck Avenue? Because *Oscar's* grill-broils its sumptuous grease-drenched burgers!

So who in hell do these pompous and pretentious prima donnas think they're frickin' kidding with their very, very bad jokes??? Grease's wide-spreading, winning appeal is quite simple really: good food, low prices, **NO PRETENTION!**

So forget all your pipe dreams about going for the gold—just go for the ecstasy-evoking grease and grime instead!

Lest we forget: hot dogs at **Top Dog**, closer to tawdry Telegraph Avenue, are **TOPS**—top-drawer and top-notch!

Take your pick then—depending on your mood—about which dingy dump's grease you prefer on the spur of your grease–dilemma–dripping moment!

We miss **Yorkshire Fish&Chips**—another dingy dive on opulent Shattuck Avenue that used to deep-fry its equally delicious grease-soaked fish and chips deep inside what could've been a tight London call box!

We even miss those other nearby shut-down, chain-style paragons and pillars of grease: **Burger King** and **KFC!!!**

Pasand Madras Cuisine. Indian industriousness marks this going concern—an "authentic ethnic" restaurant bound up tight with its notoriously grasping and greedy owner's local real estate enterprise and profiteering slumlord operation: **Reddy Realty!**

Gullible, squandering Bog-Bug spendthrifts assist both to wallow in clannish wealth! Don't patronize *skinflintism!*

It took the deaths of two young girls in a gas-ignited explosion and fire to prompt the Bog's ruling self-righteous Establishment to finally convict and incarcerate the Reddy slumlord for illegally importing from India adolescent girls for sex and slave labor. Long since the mid-80s I had personally observed the slumlord lei-surely sauntering all over the "downtown" Bog on late-night strolls with pubescent girls hanging on each arm like sugar daddy granddaughters! It took the New Mil-lennium for the sanctimonious Bog Establishment to figure out and get wise to the skinflint's shameless and salacious shenanigans.

It's a shoddy episode much akin to the Johnny–come–lately *Wives and Mothers of Berkeley Against Prostitution* who only quite belatedly berated and bad-gered the *Normandy Massage Parlor* at Haste Street and Shattuck Avenue for being a brothel and a "front for prostitution." Hookers clad in cheek-kissing skirts and stiletto heels have passed through the revolving door of that whorehouse for as many years as lecher Reddy has exploited underaged immigrant slave-girls. Only recently did hypocritical Bog-Bugs disavow their denial and pretend to take any notice let alone any action!

Poulet.   Let's cut the crap and pretension, *OKAY???!!!*

Neither "upscale" nor "sophisticated" as the *"good life"* guide's sophistry pretends this puny place is a frickin' chicken *delicatessen*—nothing more, nothing less—so forget cramming all your eggs into that over-crowded and overpacked basket trying so desperately to make it something else! *JEEZ!*

Sante Fe Bar&Grill.   This ostentatiously gar-ish and gaudy place("an oasis of LA-style glamour" the *"good life"* guide gushes)is where those younger pampered Iranian exiles haunting *Cafe Strada* start out working as penguin-suited waiters while chas-ing and salivating after their prospective "green card" brides—overcredulous women over-susceptible to shal-low, smooth-tongued and falsely-flattering drool and drivel!

With what the City•*Stupid* guide terms the "feel of a supper club" it's equally popular with people hiring stretch limos to make a grandiose display and spectacle—likely because it's one of those places few and far between in the Bog with the space off the smutty stretch of west University Avenue where limos can smoothly park far from the sanctimoniously scornful stares of the "in-town" puppet-ically correct watchdogs!

Saul's Restaurant&Delicatessen. The only thing about this parody of a supposed New York-style deli in the north Bog that successfully simulates the real thing is its snooty service which is just about as snotty as its food stinks!

Skates On The Bay. This may be *the* fad food place to sail(along with washed out, hypothermia-afflicted wind-surfers!)to on the Bog marina but it's renowned more for its so-called "breathtaking waterfront view"(the *"good life"* guide), or its "dead-on dazzling view of the Golden Gate"(the City•*Stupid* guide)or even "stunning view over the bay"(the *Insider's* guide)than its over-rated fish dishes—named as it is after the long-lost and unlamented *skate* fish which is presently **EXTINCT** in the frickin' bay! And with good reason: the luridly dull, muddy, murky and frickin' **POLLUTED** bay is more accurately, correctly and precisely described as breath-**CHOKING** than breath-taking!

This pretentious place doesn't permit bayview-aspiring patrons to reserve window tables in advance. Beside the point if you're expecting to view the distant *Golden Gate* since their window tables don't come equipped with *telescopes* anyway!

Spenger's Fresh Fish Grotto. A fad hold-over on 4th Street from 1890 whose seafood even the *"good-life"* guide admits is "overrated and overcooked"—not to mention over-priced!

It epitomizes as well the classic Bog bail-out story: in the late 1990s its greedy employee union briefly forced it to go belly-up like a suffocated *skate* fish until Bill McCormick and Doug Schmick from Portland or Seattle, depending on the most unreliable source, bailed it out with a $5 million-dollar "renovation" which still left all that maritime junk which the City•*Stupid* guide christens "nautical doodad decorations" cluttering and littering its sprawling walls.

Do we even want to go there when you can wait for up to a frickin' full hour just to set foot through the frickin' front door? *NAH!*

Stuffed Inn. This unduly under-rated sit-down deli on Euclid Avenue in the Bog north of Cal Campus with private wooden booths is where you find and over-gorge yourself on the most scrumptious and liberally over-stuffed sandwich in all the Bog. There as an angel of mine used to put it you can really *"STUFF IT UP!"*

Likewise the hospitable Persian proprietor at **Cafe Rio** on Center Street at the foot of Cal campus serves up truly fresh and hefty deli-style sandwiches.

Yogurt Park. Paying a discreet visit to this closet corner shop is always eminently amusing—if nothing else for the cheap entertainment value of watching priggish and puffed-up punks barely out of puberty peddling yogurt to blaring hard rock and heavy metal like they were brokering bonds at the frickin' stock exchange!

Skip that insipidly bland yogurt anyway and head out for *Mrs. Field's Cookies* to feast sumptuously on some real, unadulterated and "authentic" chocolate chip-, *Heath* bar- or even *Snickers*-flavored *ICE CREAM* along with some piping-hot, sugar-saturated coffee.

CHAPTER FIVE: ARTS OF THE ABSURD & ACTS OF FOLLY IN THE BOG

"From the outset, the area's natural beauty, as well as a local tolerance for a wide spectrum of human behavior, has drawn artists to the East Bay. Add to this atmosphere the stimulation and high standards of one of the world's great universities, and the result is a rich visual, scientific, and historic opportunity for visitors."—the City•*Stupid* Guide

JOSEPH COVINO JR

ARTSY-FARTSY QUACKERY IN THE BOG

As for enjoying "arts and entertainment"—bars, clubs, movie theaters, performing arts, spectator spots and "live" as opposed to dead music—in the backward, barbaric, butt-**UGLY** Bog of Berkeley there's generally very little to say or suggest except: make haste to **HURRY UP** and **GO TO SAN FRANCISCO!!!**

Since presumably there's no music anywhere that hasn't come from or out of one culture or another somewhere I've yet to figure out what pompous, pretentious and puppet-ically correct Bog-Bugs mean by *"multicultural music!"*

Another equally pompous and pretentious puppetically correct buzzword is *"alternative"* arts! *Alternative* to **WHAT?** What, what, what??? If these besotted Bog-Bugs would bend their beveled brains just the tiniest wee bit then they'd readily realize that **EVERY-THING**—without exclusion—is an "alternative" to **EVERYTHING ELSE!!! JEEZ!**

But no, they're *SO* avant garde, *SO* "cutting edge," *SO* deviate and different, *SO* "edgy," *SO* special(or so they misguidedly think!). Yeah, right: so much so that so **FEW** want to turn out to see much less hear them!

Alternative reminds me of those punk snot-nosed kids deliberately and on purpose wearing their baseball caps on their heads ass-**BACKWARDS!** So long as they're stupidly doing that I'm of strong opinion that they should forcibly be compelled to walk all around and all over the frickin' Bog ass-**BACKWARDS** as well! That's **SHITTING** edge—not *"cutting"* edge! "Living on the edge of the continent," Elizabeth Farnsworth of the *Jim Lehrer News Hour* waxes wistful, "which means being on other edges, too." Yeah, like the toilet's edges!

BERKELEY (HIGH SCHOOL AUDITORIUM) COMMUNITY THEATER

Speaking of buzzwords, bywords and misnomers the most misnamed place in all the frickin' Bog is without doubt the: *Berkeley Community Theater!*—what the "good life" guide puffs up as a "hefty venue" for sizable stage performances and concerts!

Yes, **HEFTY**—as in *hefty* bag? As in plump and portly performers? What, what, what???

And by the way, **VENUE** is a frickin' legal term referring to a crime scene or court jurisdiction!

For the longest time, though, I never knew even where the **VENUE** of the frickin' *"Berkeley Community Theater"* was! I can't even count how ever so many times confused, confounded and comatose-looking outsiders and strangers, wandering and roaming mindlessly, aimlessly, all around the main post office building but a corner away on Allston Way on some forbiddingly ominous evening would ask me: "Where's the *Berkeley Community Theater?"*(much like those bothersome visitors who'll pester you for directions to the frickin' mis-named *Greek Theatre* on Piedmont Avenue to attend the latest redundant *Gypsy Kings* concert if you happen to be laying out on the lawn across from *Cafe Strada* during "summer" trying to soak up some sun—though as even the *Insider-Out* guide admits, "this seems to happen less than it once did!").

And I could never accurately answer them back for so far as I knew: besides the over-pretentious **Berkeley Rep** on nearby Addison Street there was no theatre of even any remote note in the immediate neighborhood. For the longest time then I never knew where the frick this secret, clandestine, classified and restricted-area Bog-Bug base and compound of a *"community theater"* was or could be!

Imagine what a supreme letdown I suffered when to my bitter, sad and shocking disappointment and dismay I finally found out that the *"Berkeley Community Theater,"* so-called, was the frickin' high school **AUDITORIUM** of nearby ramshackle and run-down but more recently renovated *Berkeley High!!!*

"It adjoins Berkeley High School," the *Insider's* guide mendaciously minces. It doesn't adjoin—it's firmly ensconced on campus! "The seats aren't especially plush," the guide apologizes further, "but it's easier to stay awake that way." That should clue you in about the not–so–class acts booked there!

Bog-Bug bosses *desperately* need to rename the place at least so that outsiders and strangers could readily find it—to rightfully suit if nothing else its true station in the grand scheme of things!

BERKELEY REPERTORY THEATER(B.R.T.)

"Y ou don't have to look far to see something dramatic, compelling, or foolish on the streets of this city," gushes the *"good life"* guide. "Nonetheless, there's no shortage of actual staged theater productions. Berkeley Repertory Theater is the crown jewel of the local scene. The Rep is one of the country's top regional theaters, frequently showered with accolades and awards. They feature new works and what they call 'reinvigorated classics,' which sometimes bear little resemblance to the original piece which inspired them."

Yep, you don't have to go far at all to see something idiotic, moronic, retarded or downright stupid go down on the smutty streets of the backward, barbaric, butt-**UGLY** Bog all right!

"It may present the classics a new way," mendaciously minces the *Insider's* guide.

Never mind the conspicuously **UNNATURAL** pomposity and pretentiousness of this supposedly "progressive" playhouse which routinely butchers, dismembers and massacres beyond any and all recognition classic plays supposedly revamped and so "reinvigorated"—as if those classic plays *needed* reinvigorating; as if the **Rep** was even *qualified* to *attempt* to reinvigorate them!

But when night after insufferable night you're wondering what the frick is the frickin' attraction between roughly the hours of 7:30pm–10:30pm because you happen to live in some hovel in the *"downtown"* Bog but you can find no frickin' place to park your frickin' car: then you can rightfully thank(or blame)all those nice elderly folks driving in from miles around to patronize the **Rep**—in a worthwhile but mostly futile effort to enliven, exhilarate and "reinvigorate" their vale of years—for filling and taking up with their cars all the *"downtown"* Bog's centrally located parking spaces!

And personally I'm *SO* frickin' glad and grateful that that past female director of the **Rep** finally **MOVED ON** to Seattle or someplace so if for no other reason: we'll no longer have to suffer her exhibitionist and self-indulgent photo-op poses for the local weekly *Excess* cameras for which she habitually wore spongy shirts to flagrantly display her sagging, bra-*less* breasts! God only knows **WHY!**(something of an occult mystery much akin to why vagabond **Berkeley Symphony**— headquartered in the slummy *Shattuck Avenue Apartments*—orchestra conductor "Maestro" **Kent Nagano** never varies his punchbowl hair style!!!).

Gratuitous **GROSS-OUT!**

Equally egotistical and opportunistic in the extreme is how its "artistic" directors somehow manage to exploit that theatre "venue" to showcase and impose on captive patrons their own self-composed prosaic plays!

"Sooner or later," brags the City•*Stupid* guide, "everything comes to Berkeley." Yeah, and just as expeditiously and speedily **GOES!**

"Thanks to the area's reputation as an intellectual community with citizens that are as culturally fine-tuned as they are insatiable," its puffery persists, "the East Bay is never short on performing arts...In fact, you might say that the East Bay, a small city with high cosmopolitan standards, still considers itself a kind of

Athens."

HA, HA!! The Bog's got to be the Munchkin–and–Philistine capital of the globe—more akin to the *pit of Acheron* and the *Stygian*(not *Strawberry*)creek of **Hades** than to Athens!

And if its "indigenous" inhabitants had any "taste" at all they'd live someplace—anyplace—else!

ICELAND

Fleeting mention is made of this ice-skating rink on Milvia Street as an "amusement" in the south Bog.

Well, take then this amusing word of warning: this hoodlum hangout could very well but a lot more correctly be renamed **CRIMELAND!**

Not only has the personal property of patrons been hijacked from both inside(from both the bleachers and "rumpus room")and outside(from parked cars), not only have cars been hijacked from the place, but patrons too have themselves been hijacked—and sometimes murdered(as in some instances *ICED!*)!

It's a charming, crime-ridden "neighborhood" **Iceland** is situated in, you see, and about which the Bog remains deeply in **DENIAL:** so use **THE CLUB**—or at least carry a club with you should you so stupidly go there!

"Family-friendly" the City•*Stupid* guide calls it. Family-**FATAL** is more like it!

"Ice-skating in the mild, Mediterranean East Bay?" the *Insider's* guide wistfully fantasizes.

Ice-*expiring* and ice-*extinction* on the ice on the *rink*(rather than brink)of *death* in the incessantly icy cold of the Bog is the cold, hard reality!

Unknown "local columnists and authors" Mal and Sandra Sharpe list the "Berkeley Ice Skating Rink" as one of their "top 10 offbeat favorites." They need to leave their purse, wallet or any other "valuables" un-attended there for any length of time to experience some bodacious "offbeat" *theft!* I *dare* them!

UC ART MUSEUM

Fleeting mention is made of this Cal museum which supposedly is full of **BULL**—or what the *"good life"* guide gloats is "cutting-edge modern art!" Translation: "art" foisted on an unsuspecting public which no one either knows or cares about!

"A striking work of art itself," the City•*Stupid* guide equivocates.

"The major building walls and floor are cast gray concrete," likewise equivocates the *Insider's* guide, "giving it a utilitarian look...Fans call it rugged, utilitarian. Critics say it's brutish. At night a neon streak gives the facade a rakish look."

An exercise in utter futility and infertility is more functionally accurate!

Along with **Wurster Hall**(ironically Cal's architecture school of "environmental design")this "art museum," so-called, is arguably one of the most unsightly and butt-**UGLIEST** structures on Cal campus—specially considering the significant and substantial symbols of human civilization and culture such buildings are supposed to represent!

As Cal's sorest of eyesores both buildings rightfully qualify as outright **TRAVESTIES** of architecture!

CRUDDY CINEMA

With the exceptional exception of the wide-screen *California Cinema Center* on Kittredge Street what typifies commercial blockbuster movie theaters in the Bog are super-small screens and super-sorry sound—and what's worse the rowdy, rambunctious and unruly mobs that typically patronize them: hooligan gangs of groupies from *Film 101* class, misguidedly thinking they're so cool, hip and sophisticated that they have to boister-ously cackle, giggle and laugh **IN FRICKIN' UNI-SON IN ALL THE WRONG FRICKIN' PLACES** throughout the entire flick, drowning out dialogue and music and so spoiling it for everybody else!

What I like to do when this occurs is to loudly imitate and impersonate the grating braying of an irate mule to soundly signal to them what arrant **ASSES** they sound and most likely look like!

And typically enough they greatly get the frickin' message!

People's Republic of Berzerkeleyites flocked in frick-in' droves to watch the hugest and most outrageous film **HOAX** imaginable ever perpetrated upon the movie-going public since Orson Welles with his reading of H.G. Wells' *War of the Worlds* gulled thousands of the radio-listening public in 1938 into believing Earth was under attack by invading martians: the mockumentary *Blair Witch Project!* **TYPICAL!** But if you hon-estly thought those small piles of rocks on the ground, those twisted twigs hanging from the treetops or any of that stomach-churning hand-jive jack-off camera-work was the least bit shocking or *"scary"*(rather than mind–and–butt–numbing *DULL*)then, I'm sorry, *YOU* are frickin' *SCARY* as well as *RETARDED!!!*

PACIFIC FILM ARCHIVE AND PARAMOUNT AND PARKWAY SPEAKEASY THEATERS

Never mind the most obnoxiously, most obscenely and most outlandishly cryptic, esoteric and outright *OBSCURE* films that few people know or even care about missing, much less seeing, but which typically screen at pretentiously artsy-fartsy "rep" theaters like *Act One/Two*(that "best local venue for art and foreign films," boasts the *"good life"* guide)on Center Street in the Bog—outside which its scruffy punk flunkys frequently huddle in an antsy circle on the smutty sidewalk in the cold, elegantly attired in their snappy hip-slipping grunge gear, chain-smoking themselves into early graves while rabidly flapping their decaying gums about the brewing Bog "revolution" which, in spite of all their self-deluded wishful thinking, never, *EVER* arrives! Most of this grubby bunch of loafers and losers are unemployed hold-overs duly bounced from the now-defunct stone-seated *UC Theater* on University Avenue that most predictably folded due to persistently piss-poor programming!

Then there was that comparably pretentious *Fine Arts Cinema*(the one-time smut "art house")that briefly came at us on Shattuck Avenue in the south Bog with yet more "diverse" and "unusual" film programming(as *IF* the Bog hadn't *ENOUGH* of *IT* already!)—meaning yet *MORE* unknown, unnoted, unsung and unheard-of films *NOBODY* knows or cares about—before it was blessedly **DEMOLISHED** to make way for some urgently needed gentrified neighborhood apartments!

That gravest and most outrageously blasphemous, sacrilegious and unforgivable SIN committed by both the "world famous"(over-exaggerates the "good life" guide)*Pacific Film Archive*(which in distant times past was sunk stealthily beneath Cal's *University Art Museum*)and Oakland's landmark *Paramount* theaters, though, is that idiotic, imbecilic, inane, moronic and retarded prohibition against serving within them any concession stand snacks or refreshments like candy, popcorn and soda!!!

If that weren't perverse, perverted and profane enough the "Archive" frequently forces its captive audience to sit arduously through some tedious and tiresome "lecture"—in its blatant attempt to bore you to tears or put you to sleep before the frickin' flick even screens!

Little wonder that it moved across the street on Bancroft Way into a makeshift, aluminum prefab Quonset–hut–style structure with a lecture–hall–style "auditorium" with distressingly uncomfortable classroom–style–seats.

Such a schlocky set-up amounts to nothing less than movie *MISERY!*

Oakland's *Paramount* forces its captive audience to sit arduously through some wearisome wheel–of–

fortune gaming–giveaway("like gift certificates to local restaurants," gushes the City•*Stupid* guide)before
"movie classics" screen—an interminably prolonged
burlesque parody called *"Dec–O–Win!"* Meanwhile
their puritanically stern-faced ushers prowl and patrol
the theater aisles hot on the police-surveillance scent of
patrons sucking on tic-tacs!

At the dingy *Parkway Speakeasy* movie dive in
Oakland the exact opposite extreme prevails—you can
sit in ramshackle chairs and couches and at least eat
to your heart's(and gut's)indigestive discontent everything from sandwiches to pizza!

But to view the more popular "cult classic" flicks
you'll have to suffer the theater's buffoonish program-
mer, Will *"the Thrill"* Viharo, while he compels his captive audience to endure not just his *"Big Wheel spin"*
but, worse, his powerfully *UN*-funny stand-up slap-
stick schtick!

This creepy court jester should re-christen himself
Will the *DULL!* and finally get over it and give it up!
After years of imposing on captive audiences his weari-
some routine and flopping royally he still just doesn't
GET IT: he's a frickin' droning *BORE!!!*

As in frickin' *BORING!!!* So just *GET LOST, GET
OFF* the frickin' stage and screen the frickin' flick!

Oakland mayor Jerry *"Moonbeam"* Brown lists
these theaters as "reasons(he)wouldn't live anywhere
but Oakland." Perhaps such *explains* much!

SPECTATOR SPORTS

As for sitting stupidly in some stupendous
sports stadium somewhere and watching
some soporific spectator sport: that has got to
be the single most monumentally *MONOTO-*

NOUS AND TEDIOUS FRICKIN' THING TO DO IN ALL THE WHOLE WIDE WORLD—so we don't even wanna go there!!!

ARTSY-FARTSY DISTRICT

Epitomizing the Bog's most absurdly pretentious Arts of the Absurd is its so-called "Downtown Arts District On Addison Street," where puffs the official visitors guide: "The pedestrian experience is enhanced by a streetscape with public art." For that matter the "pedestrian experience" is decidedly *endangered* since that supposedly "unique sidewalk"(red brick sidewalk "poetry panels")becomes incredibly and dangerously slippery—and so a pedestrian hazard—when the least bit wet or moist from rain or fog.

An even more offensive hazard to both human eyesight and sensitivity are those unsightly **Addison Windows**, so-called, containing some of the most abominable and abhorrent artistic atrocities imaginable.

These Art Display Windows Are Dedicated to the Memory of Peter T. Babcock, 1951-1991, Graphic Artist, Champion of Public Art and President of the Berkeley Civic Arts Commission, 1982-1986—gold plaque

Wherever he is poor P.T. Babcock must be turning over in his proverbial grave!

Then there's that craggy and gnarled eyesore—a tall misshapen lump of "Dutch ceramic stoneware and French and German porcelain clays"—perched high atop a block pedestal at Addison Street on Shattuck Square.

Titled *'S—Herto Gen Bosch, 2003* it looks literally like a towering turd some colossal creature pooped out and dumped bolt upright right there on the sidewalk. Indeed it would be utterly undistinguished were it not for the copious birdshit droppings it's constantly pelted with!

It boggles the mind that the Bog's sage city fathers would even commission John Toki to produce such a piece of crap for display anyplace in public view!

Then there's that gigantic monstrosity of a red-painted steel **TUNING FORK** designated as an "art-work"—titled *Earth Song, 2002*—and erected smack dab in the middle of the pedestrian crosswalk at Center Street and Shattuck Avenue.

That's a frickin' **APPARATUS**—*NOT* a frickin' piece of *"artwork!"*

JOSEPH COVINO JR

CHAPTER SIX: MONEYCHANGERS IN THE BOG

"Still happily out of step with the rest of America, Berkeley and Oakland have mostly resisted the lure of malls."— City•*Stupid* guide

BITS OF THE BOG:
THE HALF-NAKED GUY

One distant "summer" Sunday on one of the rarer, more unusually lukewarm and somewhat sunny days in the Bog—the 20th of July 1996—I paused in front of *Hillel* Jewish student center at 2736 Bancroft Way on my way to run at the *Clark-Kerr* dirt track(at the easterly top of Dwight Way)to strip down to my gym shorts, shedding just my shirt. A very friendly Latino gardener named Javier working there outside came up to me, grinning widely and jesting at first that he thought I was the infamous and notorious *Andrew Martinez*, aka *"The Naked Guy"*—and that I was about to take off my shorts too, stripping down to my bare essentials as it were.

"No, sorry," I apologized, "I'm the *HALF*-naked guy!"

Which in the Bog feels strange and weird enough, especially without a sandy, sunny, ocean-bound beach to lay out on!

So what **IS** it anyway with these nudist "activists," so-called, posing for the Bog that most momentous, all-arresting question—to dress up or to dress down—or as the *"good life"* guide equivocated: "To clothe or not to clothe—in Berkeley, that is the question."

Now personally I'm a classic liberal, abiding by a simple live–and–let–live philosophy, which naturally infers a personal *responsibility* to at least try to avoid infringing on, offending or otherwise violating the legitimate rights and freedoms of others without being an *imposition* on anyone. That differs radically from pretentious, puppet-ically correct progressives, trying relentlessly and irresponsibly at every turn to inflict

145

and force down everyone else's throat their entire distorted outlook and viewpoint! That's not tolerance but tyranny!

So whether these nudist "activists" are shameful or shameless as such I really could care less. Nor do I care whether they exercise their supposed "freedom" to strip bare and run naked as such, depending on *where* they do it—only they fail to exercise their freedom *responsibly* when they infringe on the right of onlookers to be free *from* seeing that often unsightly sight of them striding in the nude! Their self-centered and self-indulgent stripping, though, most inconsiderately and thoughtlessly gives nobody any *choice* or *freedom* to decide who—or what—they might see exposed!

After all, aren't pretentious puppet-ically correct progressives supposed to be real **BIG** on the "issue" of free choice???

Paraphrasing how one comedian most succinctly put it: thanks for sharing but gimme a break! Don't show me more about you than I may necessarily need—or *want*—to know!

That should be the onlooking watcher's right and free choice!

Partial nudity is, besides, far more enticing and sensuous anyway: keeping up at once that desirable sense of mystery as well as that tantalizing and titillating *hint* of possible pleasure and delight to come—should we freely *choose* and be *chosen* to go there!

Arguably you could even wish for a freer choice whether to see even some of the faces much less genitals of certain passerby. But at least the *eyes* are supposed to be windows to the human soul—about which preferably we do want to know more perhaps than about some stranger's grotesque(and frequently deficient)sexual and reproductive anatomy!

BUYERS AND SELLERS IN THE BOG

Now I'd never even dream to presume to tell you, dear readers, where to go to shop for goods and services in the Bog. But I will offer you this small sampling of tangible tips for the very suitable sake of: *BUYER BEWARE!*

BANKS

Bank of America. It comes as absolutely no surprise at all that this thieving, predatory bank is reputedly California's "largest"—it charges the costliest and most exorbitant(if not extortionate!)fees for every conceivable service—quite apart from its flat monthly statement fees or its automated "self-service" calling system fees it'll clip you for upwards of $32 a pop simply for its "non-sufficient funds"(*NSF*)fees(just to mention a scant few)! Try instead *Washington Mutual* with its perfectly *fee-free* monthly checking with its $1 minimum deposit!

BOOKSTORES

Half-Price Books. Now nearby *Moe's Books* has reputedly been called the "yeastiest center of intellectual ferment" in the Bog—whatever the frick *that* means!

But in the brain-blighting, pretentious, pseudo-intellectual capital of the world the greediest and most grasping center of both book-bilking and money-milking is *Half-Price*—misusing its misleading name as its lame-ass, piss-poor excuse to pettily pay out a puny

PITTANCE—or those proverbial peanuts—for any used books you might try to sell or trade there!

And all the while at *Half-Price* their mug will be smug as they rook you for your books!

CDS, DVDS, RECORDS, TAPES&VIDEOS

Amoeba Music. And the very same holds true for this CD, DVD, record, tape and video store—the founders of which vowed to show local Bog-Bugs the least "attitude" when it first opened up for business. Now since it's been long-established it naturally most shamelessly displays the *UTMOST* attitude—not only in fleecing sellers of their used and disused trade-ins but most blatantly boasting about it amongst their cronies behind your back after you've passed through as well!

And then at closing time throughout the store's cross and cocky cattle calls to its customers sassy staffers will have the brazen-faced gall to whine babyishly to you about the overlong hours those poor, bitter Bog-Bug babies have had to work toiling so laboriously moving all those weightless musical wares—just as you're about to buy a frickin' *basketful* of merchandise costing enough to pay their entire frickin' week's wages with the money *you* worked overlong hours to earn to frickin' spend there!!!

Amoeba Music, gloats the City•*Stupid* guide, "is the least chainlike and the most Berkeley." And as its name perfectly implies it will fully engulf your wallet and swallow up every last almighty dollar in it!

Even under his Svengali-gaze *Rasputin's* is far friendlier and more hospitable!

COPY SHOPS

Krishna Copy. Copies there are the dirt-cheapest and its energetic and hardworking staff is fast on their feet, super-efficient and conscientiously strive to satisfy!

MUSIC STORES

Tupper&Reed(Blessedly Out–of–Business). And the very same holds very true for this musical instrument store on Shattuck Avenue in the "downtown" Bog: *T&Reed* pays only ***CHICKEN FEED*** to sellers of good- and even mint-conditioned musical instruments!

As for their spurious claim that they stock the "largest selection of sheet music in Northern California" I seriously suggest that you check out in San Francisco ***Byron Hoyt Sheet Music Service***, which makes good on that claim!

One past employee duly dubbed *T&Reed*: ***"SUFFER&BLEED!"***

OFFICE SUPPLIES

Alko Office Supply. ***Radston's Office Supply Co.*** on Shattuck Avenue in the northward Bog, exaggerates the *"good life"* guide, "has everything you need to get your desk and your life together."

Radston's is hardly *rad!* But if you have to go there to get your "life" together then you've got to be the most lame-ass loser of the most mesomorphic order!

For getting your desk-act together, though, forget those indifferent and impertinent staffers at ***Radston's*** and head for the far friendlier and more helpful folks at ***Alko Office Supply*** in the "downtown" Bog instead!

SUPERMARKETS

Safeway(Northside). And speaking of friendly and helpful employees the absolute and arrant *BEST* supermarket in all the Bog is the northside *Safeway*—situated just beyond the gastritis–and–gourmet gulch on Shattuck Avenue—the most pleasant and pleasurable place to grocery shop!

Even well before that shambles of a *Safeway* on Oregon Street in the south Bog blessedly shut up shop in November 1994 I would *HIKE* a very long way back and forth between my hovel in the south Bog and the far superior and spotless northside Safeway, trudging and lugging on foot bagfuls of groceries just to *AVOID* footing it to that shabby and seedy southside store!

Editors of the *East Bay Excess* once called that gutted and stripped supermarket in the south Bog the *"Best Business Opportunity Going Begging!"*

Where in the whole frickin' Bog do these wittily witless court jesters live anyhow???

Anyone living in the south Bog knows full well, after all, that "neighborhood" thieves and thugs, giving not a damn about faddish organic foods sold nearby at those fad stores(*Berkeley Bowl* and *Whole Foods*), both looted the store and bullied shoppers—in spite of obnoxious and overbearing *"courtesy clerks"*—making their supermarket slum as unsavory as it was unprofitable!!!

Any *TAKERS*, the *Excess* asked ineptly!

What rational or sane business investors worth their health-minded profit margins would even *THINK* about so *STUPIDLY* taking it???!!! None did. None would.

In the end that particular crackpot conundrum concluded with a typical, hypocritical, artificially contrived and doctored solution: a big Bog-bankrolled ***BAIL-OUT!***

Tax–propped–and–supported Bog-Bug bosses charitably and liberally subsidized the expedient move of ***Berkeley Bowl*** from its old dilapidated bowling alley barn across the street to its present freshly remodeled and renovated—and reconverted—structure: the old run-down ***Safeway*** building! Lettuce is lettuce but those oh–so–hip–and–sophisticated Berzerkeley-ites will stupidly stand for hours in tediously long lines at ***Berkeley Bowl*** to get the exact same salad leaves but still witlessly thinking the whole time that they're getting something *special!* Frickin' *incredible!*

At the all-night College Avenue ***Safeway*** you'll get continuously accosted by persistent panhandlers.

At the all-night Solano Avenue ***Safeway*** in Albany you'll get accosted by over-presumptuous ruffian stock clerks who ***THINK*** they're tough-guys!

Go to ***Andronico's*** only if you really relish throwing good money after bad for the very same but excessively *overpriced* supermarket stock found everyplace else.

The Main
UNITED STATES
POST OFFICE

Most Special Mention

In the entire Bog the most consistently courteous, friendly and helpful federal public servant used to be a career postal professional named **ROD A. DIAZ**—bar ***NONE!*** Unfortunately for the Bog "community" he's long-since but most deservedly retired!

Quite an abnormal aberration for the Bog this diligent postal expert would take the time and trouble to take pains to bend over backwards to knock himself out to move heaven and earth to do anything, everything and whatever he could to kindly **HELP** you to most efficiently and expeditiously to take care and dispose of with full dispatch your most seriously pressing postal business!

Dramatically contrast him with your typical Bog-Bug civil servant: deaf, dumb(mostly), pert, rude, imperiously ill-mannered and **S-L-O-W** as frickin' molasses in both perception and reaction to any living life-form of public contact!

By their supremely condescending attitude these other monkeys in mortal suits act like it's a colossal inconvenience even to listen to much less to publicly help or serve anyone!

Perfect case–in–point: two black women staffing the police station's public reception desk, sitting listlessly inside their muffled glass cage—inextricably and immovably **RIVETED** to their frickin' seats!

Totally and utterly **USELESS!!!**

The Downtown Berkeley YMCA

In spite of all those disingenuous, slogan-eering signs touting *"RESPECT"* plastered all over the place one group and one group alone rules and reigns supreme at this powerfully amateurish arena: the **Dorky Punk** contingent!

DORKY PUNKS abound en masse and they're

perched *everywhere!* These sappy, sassy, smart-al-ecky staffers(otherwise known as adolescent tyrants–in–training–for–developing–world–countries high on control freak-style power-trips!)*overrun* the front reception service desk, the so-called "activity areas," locker rooms and even the swimming pool lifeguard stations! And they get away with carrying on with their adolescent antics with the whole-hearted blessing, cod-dling and pampering of the irresponsible adolescent-acting "adult" administration. Then come closing time these dorky drones will harpingly mope and moan and pout and shuffle around whining about how long and how hard they've had to "work" all day—lounging and slouching to "boom box" noise in their cushioned re-clining chairs! Even more pathetic are their supposed "adult" supervisors who chime in so childishly right along with them. Then again: what else would you ex-pect from members of their *"union."*

Come **ON!** Get **REAL!** These infantile idlers and loafers don't know what real work **IS** but sorely need to **LEARN!**

One—just one—long day out on the road with a *Cal-Trans* crew would thoroughly both educate and cure them!

There's one chubby, blonde, bratty, foot–stomp-ing, hands–on–her–hips, huffing–and–puffing, tem-per–tantrum–throwing little girl staffer barely out of puberty there who's so bitterly frustrated about being such a twirpy twit that she's prematurely menopausal and persistently mis-pronounces her name unlike it's spelled—much like Sade(*Shar*-Day!).

Then there's this long-time aging, graying, short, runty and wrinkled gaffer-staffer who habitually ogles, gawks and drools after younger female members like he's some hunky stud rather than the pipsqueak pervert he really is. Truly pathetic!

What this **YMCA's** corps of punks can't grasp is the excruciatingly simple concept that adult members work hard to pay their membership dues(which in turn pay the juvenile staff's wages)and go to the gymnasium to relax and refresh themselves—not just to train or work out. What adult members don't work hard to pay for is to be rudely bossed or condescended to or otherwise treated with discourtesy and disrespect by smart-alecky, dorky and uppity punk kids who don't know what real work or hardship is!

That's just how this bizarre branch of the **YMCA** operates: with hypocritical *"RESPECT!"* But public *service* staff exist for the convenience and satisfaction of the **PATRONS** served—not the other way around!

Speaking of a singular lack of respect that's precisely what you'll see most habitually practiced by the punks pretending to "work out" at Cal's **Recreational Sports Facility(RSF).**

"If you're unfazed by the proximity of young, strong, undergraduate athletes," over-exaggerates the City•*Stupid* guide, "this Olympic-size facility offers large helpings of every kind of exercise."

Athletes? You've **GOT** to be kidding! What frickin' *athletes?* Hordes of scrawny Asian kids who haven't the first or remotest clue about how to correctly work out, much less about training etiquette, make up the largest contingent over-populating and over-running the **RSF.**

Thoughtless and inconsiderate in the extreme, the punks run amuck, hoarding weights they don't use(like it's a reserve library rather than a gymnasium)and neglecting to return the weights they do *mis*-use to the racks once they're done dragging and dawdling with the equipment(like they're waiting for librarians to return books to the shelves). Utterly oblivious and ob-noxious!

Go to the **RSF** gym and you'll waste most of your time scavenger hunting for mislaid equipment left scattered all over the frickin' place or waiting over-long for turns at machines or stations!!!

EDWARDS TRACK STADIUM
(Cal Campus)

"Track!   Track!" is the mannered and pompous outcry you'll sometimes hear from behind your back if ever you happen to be jogging or running—during rec-reational running hours!—in this track's first, second or supposed *fast* lanes!

Well, if and whenever you do hear it—just ignore it, stand your ground and keep right on running in the lane you can rightly lay claim to *because you were running there* **FIRST!!!** And if need be tell the jerk-off boob yelping at you from behind because he haughtily expects *you* to move aside so he can pass you by in *your* running lane—as if he *owned* the frickin' lane: "Go the frick **AROUND!!!**"

After 5pm daily to dusk and beyond time and space at this track is generally *reserved*—quite fairly and justly—for **RECREATIONAL** running and **RECRE-ATIONAL** runners of whatever skill or speed!

Sooner or later though—in the face of all courtesy and civility, in spite of the signed rules posted at the track's gate *prohibiting* private training by persons or groups un-affiliated with Cal's established athletic clubs or programs—some elitist jerk-off track-boob group(like the *"East Bay Striders"*—or Stragglers!)or groupie will show up: out solely to stroke their jack-legged egos by overtaking and passing slower *recreational* runners to self-deludedly fool and prove to themselves their supposed physical prowess and superiority—especially since they're utterly unfit and unqualified to compete among truly competitive athletes!

If they can't or won't learn respect for *recreational* track rules then you can at least teach them these good manners and *recreational* track etiquette: neither your runner-up skill nor your runner-up pace automatically entitles you to ***ANY*** special or preferential track rights or privileges much less to any imaginary right–of–way in that all-sacred first or *fast* lane; nor is *any* part of the track meant at any time to be converted into your own personal or private running domain!!!

Got ***THAT???!!! Good!!!***

So, mister runner-up runner: if you can't show the slower *recreational* runner you're bootlessly trying to intimidate and impress some small ***SEMBLANCE*** of common courtesy and consideration then simply do the good and decent thing: go the frick ***AROUND***—or risk getting knocked down to the frickin' ***GROUND!!!***

VIDEO RENTALS

In true and typical Bog-Bug fashion bombastic and loud-mouthed residents of the south Bog childishly clamored and protested against **Hollywood Video** from moving into their "neighborhood" to set up shop because of its *neon*, "strip-mall" facade—for fanatical fear that it just might brush and touch up the place the tiniest little bit!

So in equally true and typical Bog-Bug form—as things turned out—a newfangled video rental store called **Reel** set up shop behind a bland beige facade in the vacant property owned and leased out by the very same company the bitter Bog-Bug babies living in the south Bog cried so vociferously about: **Hollywood Video!** Hypocritical pretention and obsession with the superficial in the extreme!

Believe it or not!!!

"Please do not make this area another Miami Beach," the *Daily **Cull*** student-recycled paper quoted one south Bog protester as pleading against the chain video rental store.

Dream ON!!!

The backward, barbaric, butt-***UGLY*** Bog of Berkeley should be so lucky to ***EVER*** look ***ANYTHING*** even ***REMOTELY*** so supremely ***SUPERIOR*** as Miami Beach!!!

BITS OF THE BOG: *JUNIOR* IN BERKELEY

As you may already well know or care less scenes from the Arnold Schwarzenegger "comedy" picture—*Junior(1994)*—were shot in and around the Bog as well as on Cal campus.

Tooting my own horn, then, I must make mention of my own break-out acting role in the movie—as a disgruntled film extra playing a news photographer milling around outside the Bog's *Bancroft Hotel* at 2680 Bancroft Way the 14th of May 1994 when the film's *Noah Banes* character(played by **dud Dracula** actor *Frank Langella*)officially presents the "world's first pregnant man!"

Well, after the announcement proves false and the *Danny DeVito* character's wife, *Angela*(played by actress *Pamela Reed*)gets out of the car instead of big-bellied **AH**-nold, watch out closely for *Yours Truly*, the Berkeley **BASHER!**—tall, dark and dashing in coat and maroon tie—shuffling and smirking among the other disappointed, dissatisfied and dispersing news reporters!

I got a great shot in that flick!

CONCLUDING ODE:
PLATO&MICHAEL CHABON

Michael Chabon's *"Special–to–the–Chron-icle"*(15 August 2004*)Ode to Berkeley* amounts to being such a powerfully ***PRO-FUSE*** piece of puffery—so mightily far-ranging in its outright ***DERANGEMENT***—I'm now of the unswerving conviction that *Pulitzer Prizes*(of which Chabon's a recipient)are either rigged or award-ed to frickin' ***RETARDS*** for churning out pure, un-adulterated ***IDIOCY!*** And it'll demand a veritable Pla-tonic dialogue to soundly rebut it. So here goes—with **MC** standing for Michael Chabon and **BB** standing for, yours truly, the one and only Berkeley ***BASHER!***

MC. "Berkeley. Where passion is married to intel-ligence, you may find genius, neurosis, madness or rap-ture. None of these is really an unfamiliar presence in the tree-lined streets of Berkeley, California."

BB. "You're royally confused, Michael. You mis-guidedly confuse passion with fanatical extremism, pseudo-intellectualism with intelligence and so ge-nius, neurosis, madness and rapture with deliberately self-inflicted stupidity, obsessiveness, paranoia and downright depression respectively. And if you haven't noticed most of the trees in the Bog are pretty frickin' scraggly!"

MC. "But it seems to me that among the many sad and homeless people who haunt Berkeley one finds an unusually high number of poets, sages, secret Napo-leons and old-fashioned prophets of doom."

BB. "Such fanciful(and shallow)romanticizing pre-cisely typifies how pretentious Bog-Bugs trivialize the already marginalized homeless population: they largely *ignore* it! A simple creative visualization most deftly demonstrates how most pretentious Bog-Bugs deal with and handle those 'sad' homeless street people lying so conspicuously but so inconveniently in the Bog's sundry smutty gutters: they **STEP RIGHT OVER THEM AND GO RIGHT ON TRUCKIN'!** And their pretentious motto while they're steppin' is: *One small step for man. One giant leap of* **PRETENTION** *for mankind!"*

MC. "I'd be willing to bet that, pound for pound, Berkeley is the most enraptured city in America on a daily basis."

BB. "Yeah, well, I'd be willing to bet that you'd roundly **LOSE** any such wager since the Bog is more accurately the most distressingly afflicted and tortured town in the entire country."

MC. "And yet I declare, unreservedly and with all my heart, that I love Berkeley, California. I can't imagine living happily anywhere else. And all of the things that drive me crazy are the very things that make this town worth knowing, worth putting up with, worth loving and working to preserve."

BB. "And I declare, equally unreservedly and with heart and soul, that your so-called 'love' is as warped and perverted as it is severely misplaced. I can imagine nothing *but* living ecstatically someplace—anyplace—else! And there's absolutely nothing whatever about the town, so-called, worth knowing and loving much less worth putting up with and preserving. In fact, it would be all well and good and for the best for the world if the whole backward, barbaric and butt-**UGLY** Bog of Berkeley were irrevocably **NUKED** from the face of the Earth!!!! Besides, come off it(that high horse!): sitting pretty as you do in a *'Berkeley Brown shingle'* exemplar, reportedly in or around opulent and insulated *Piedmont*, you don't really know what 'living' in the real Bog is like so don't even pretend that you do—at least not until you get sentenced to serving some lengthy time in the distant south(Adeline at Alcatraz streets)or west(San Pablo and University Avenues)flats of the Bog where the real Bog action is! Yes, what I strongly suspect you sorely need to get your priorities straight is to experience firsthand some good old-fashioned crime and punishment—Bog-style! Then I guarantee that you'd promptly sing a different and diametrically opposite tune!"

MC. "When the end finally comes, I believe that Berkeley will be the last town in America with the ingrained perversity to hold onto its idea of itself."

BB. "That's the saddest and most tragic reality about the Bog. The bitter 'end' has indeed already long since come to the Bog but bitter and frustrated Bog-Bugs wallow in such 'ingrained,' intransigent and deliberately self-inflicted and self-indulgent but deep *DE-NIAL* about anything and everything *real or truthful* they just don't realize it yet!!!!"

MC. "Berkeley is richer than any place I've ever lived...A business that would never thrive anywhere else, patronized by people who would never thrive anywhere else, in a city that lives and dies on the passion and intelligence, the madness and rapture, of its citizens."

BB. "Fine for you to say—you've got yours, haven't you? But you must not have lived before at very many commendable or impeccable places—either that or you must've merely *overlooked and ignored* a lot just as bitter Bog-Bugs here deliberately *disregard and deny* a lot! Native Bog-Bugs don't 'thrive'—they subsist and stagnate—and just barely at that! And if the 'city,' so-called, survives at all it's purely by the irrational

fanaticism and pseudo-intellectualism, the derangement and denial of its denizens. And the ***PARANOID
SCOWL***(not the 'suspicious frown')is their 'default fa-
cial expression.')!!!"

CHAPTER SEVEN: SUBJECTS OF PUPPET-ICALLY CORRECT CONTROVERSY —RACE, SEX, RELIGION & POLITICS

"Oakland, similar to any big city, has its mean streets. But its reputation as crime-ridden is inflated."—the City•*Stupid* guide

JOSEPH COVINO JR

YOU MOTHAFRICKIN' VISIGOTH— I'M GONNA GIT YOU, SUCKA!

Now about this tiring and tiresome **RACE** thing all I wanna know is: who in hell in our present day and age grieves, mourns or sheds any tears at all for all those natives of Italy murdered and massacred by militant and warring *VISIGOTHS???!!!*

Well, I'm mostly of Italian ancestry which by the passive, puppet-ically correct movement makes me an *I-TALIAN AMERICAN*—and so duly **PROUD** and *em-POWERED* to proclaim openly and publicly to all the world my *I-TALIAN* identity, ethnicity, culture and heritage!

Now as you may very well recall those damn, blasted Visigoths were Teutonic—or Germanic—peoples invading the Roman Empire during the third and fourth centuries! And I just think that all their vile and evil offspring of each and every succeeding generation should be *made* to **PAY**—and pay **DEARLY** and *IN-DEFINITELY*—for all the grievous and wicked wrong, injury and injustice their maliciously vicious ancestors did to my more blameless and innocent *I-TALIAN* forebears! That's fair!

For that matter I think it's high past time that descendants of these Germanic peoples—as if present-day Germans haven't been *retro*-persecuted enough by the Jews for the Nazi-instigated holocaust—should be constantly and incessantly reminded(*hounded*, really, lest either we or they frickin' forget!)by means of the media(books, movies, music, TV)just how profoundly fiendish and diabolical their ancient ancestors really were!

To really level the universal "playing field" of equality and justice, so far as that goes, I think that all *I-TALIAN AMERICANS* living in Germanic countries should get special and preferential treatment over all other fellow citizens in schools, jobs and most especially in the legal process! For *I-TALIAN AMERICANS*, then, due process of law should mean total exemption and immunity from both prosecution and punishment for violating laws applying equally to everyone else or for committing even the most heinous of violent and murderous crimes—no matter how bloodthirsty or atrocious!

Sounds silly and stupid, doesn't it? Of course—*SOUNDLY SO!* Except for the difference and disparity in *TIME* itself, though, isn't that precisely how so many *"people of color"*(contemporary *"colored people"* without the preposition!)sound today as they keep on blaming, condemning and denouncing—so wrongly—so many present-day descendants for the ever so many transgressions committed by one race of ancient ancestors against another, presumably antagonistic and opposing race of ancestors?

Talk about livin' in the frickin' past and harping on ancient history! None complain more bitterly, more indignantly, more profusely or more vociferously than Blacks and Jews complain so chronically and so clamorously about the—yes, very *real* and very *valid*—atrocities and outrages inflicted on them by the—yes, very severe—persecution and oppresion of times *PAST:* slavery and the holocaust respectively!

Honestly, though, it gets to be richly ridiculous when those whining most about distant past victimization by long bygone persecutors and oppressors are coddled, pampered, privileged, pseudo-intellectual youth—as if these present-day descendants had actually experienced, suffered and endured any of the atrocities and outrages of their victimized ancestors themselves! It gets even more ridiculous when these latter-day racial victims and whiners—even *NOW!*—accuse, blame and hold responsible the present-day descendants and generations of other, presumably hateful and hostile races for the injuries and injustices done to them by their long since *GONE*(truly, their mostly long since *DEAD!*)persecutors and oppressors!

None of this is meant to imply that any of us should forget or ignore the injuries and injustices done to us by persecutors and oppressors in times gone by—or even that we should forget or ignore those very valid and real injuries and injustices being done in our present time by present-day persecutors and oppressors! Nor should we with truth ever forget the selfless sacrifices made for our sakes and on our behalf by our most honored—or dishonored—ancestors!

What we should remember more carefully or turn our minds to more vigilantly is our commonly shared *HUMANITY*—becoming *HUMAN*-Americans more than ethnic-Americans, preoccupying ourselves more with pursuing *HUMAN*-benefitting and *HUMAN*-serving purposes than our more narrowly defined parochial, provincial and self-indulgent *SELF-INTER-ESTS!* And we should do so for those *ALIVE AND LIVING* in the here and now of today rather than for the dead and gone of yesterday's past!

If there does happen to be any fault-finding and finger-pointing to do then at least try laying the blame for injury and injustice where it most justly and rightly belongs: squarely at the door of those officers and functionaries of officialdom—of whatever arena—most abusing and misusing their public **AUTHORITY** over **HUMANITY** at large! Get it????

Now when it comes to the race thing bitter Bog-Bug bosses are persistently and perpetually in total **DENIAL** as are most puppet-ically correct groupies, especially when it comes to facing up to the fact and reality of **WHO's** committing—quite disproportionately for whatever alibi or excuse—most of the violent crime going down in the Bog and its immediate environs. And they'll likely remain in denial—in spite of the added fact and reality that far too many young lives are being lost on the Bog's bloodthirsty streets lately because teenagers have taken to **KILLING** each other right and left! And parents and teachers alike keep on blaming the nebulous "system" rather than taking some small measure of **RESPONSIBILITY** for doing **SOMETHING** about their own negligent wrongdoing!

"Berkeley, Oakland, and some of the surrounding cities have not escaped the problems that plague most of the country's metropolitan areas," admits even the apologetic *Insider's* guide. "Berkeley's rate for violent crime is slightly above average, registering 941.6 crimes per year per 100,000 people compared to the national annual average of 634.1. Oakland's rate is 2,184 crimes per 100,000 people, more than three times the national average. Richmond, another urban area with drug and poverty problems, has a rate of 1,845.5."

Everybody knows full well that those areas of Oakland and Richmond so rife with violent crime are predominantly **BLACK** but the Bog's pretentious progressives are so profoundly afraid to say the truth outright—plain and clear for all to hear. And all denial aside an annual murder rate in excess of a **HUNDRED** homicides a year is **NOT** a **NORMAL** state of affairs— or at least it shouldn't be—no matter where it is!

Facing facts and *reality* thoughtfully, critically and truthfully has nothing whatever to do with accusing, blaming, condemning, denouncing or casting any aspersions on any ethnic culture or race. Nor has it anything whatever to do with those two most chronically and habitually abused, misused and puppet-ically correct **MISNOMERS**: **RACISM** and **STEREOTYPE**— nor even with their bigoted delusions of self-important grandeur and superiority!

Simple *prejudice*(and everybody's prejudiced about something or someone in one way or another)isn't **racism**(which by definition implies a belief or feeling of *racialsuperiority*)anymorethan*generalizations*(things which are generally true)are **stereotypes**. Such terms are not inter-changeable and should stop being abused and mis-used by the pretentiously progressive!

And by the way aberrantly isolated **EXCEPTIONS** to the rule never effectively disprove generalizations—or **"STEREOTYPES!"** It's the exceptions that **PROVE** the rule!

Facing facts and *reality*, quite the contrary, does in fact have everything to do with really recognizing a problem and taking practical and realistic steps to deal with it honestly and forthrightly! So **GET OVER YOUR DENIAL AND DEAL WITH IT**, bitter Bog-Bug babies!

About one thing at least I sincerely believe the rightly respected and revered Martin Luther King Jr. was downright wrong: that as unknowing strangers to one another we should judge other people not by their skin color(which is fine)but by the *"content of their character!"* Do any of us really need or want anyone else judging the content of our character???

Far more fair, impartial, just and unbiased is judging other people—of whatever race—by their *actions, behavior and conduct*: *without* judging in terms of *we versus they!* Due to what courts would term extenuating or mitigating circumstances a person's actions, behavior and conduct aren't always reflective(or representative)of their true character.

HOW else, after all—or in what better way—can people rationally or reasonably hold any opinion or come to any conclusion about anything except through their own firsthand personal experience? ***WHAT*** else can *some* people be expected to ***PERCEIVE*** when the overwhelming ***MAJORITY*** of their firsthand personal experience shows and proves to them that, no, not all but ***MOST*** people of certain other races they meet tend to act and behave in certain offensive, obnoxious and otherwise objectionable ways?

WHO then is really ***RESPONSIBLE*** for certain ***PERCEPTIONS*** of certain racial *"stereotypes"* and negative images—the perceiver or the perceived?

Well, when violence, vulgarity and incivility invariably exemplify and typify the actions, behavior and conduct of certain people ***EN MASSE*** of whatever race or ethnicity—so chronically, so consistently, so habitually, so regularly, so repetitiously in countless incidents and endless episodes over and over, time and time again— then it's high past time to ***CALL A SPADE A SPADE*** and, further, to ***CALL TO ACCOUNT*** the perceived ***VICTIMIZERS*** rather than the perceiving victims and, more, hold ***THEM*** answerable for the images and reputations that only they alone create and perpetuate for themselves! That means shifting the burden of perceptions to where it more fairly, justly and rightly belongs by holding those really **RESPONSIBLE** for both generating and sustaining their own more unsavory images and reputations(**BY** their actions, behavior and conduct!).

Blacks generally suffer an "image" problem but it's solely of their own making. Out of one corner of their mouths they'll whine clamorously about the supposed white "slave mentality" and about "racial profiling" of them as criminals, gang members or as being unduly indigent and disadvantaged. Out of the other corner of their mouths—in the very selfsame breath—they'll whine equally clamorously about being marginalized, underprivileged and "trapped in poverty." Then they'll demand not only apologies for ancient abuses(which they never suffered)but also reparations and other hand-outs like automatically assured "affirmative action" or material "privileges" they've neither earned nor worked for. And then they'll typically threaten with violence anyone daring to *"offend"* them by contradicting or otherwise objecting to their not only unreasonable but utterly unjust demands.

If blacks really and truly want to improve their collective image and other people's reasonable perceptions of them then they need quite simply to *stop* committing violent crimes so rampantly, *stop* joining gangs so rampantly and *stop* playing the impoverished victims–demanding–hand-outs so rampantly. It's just that plain and simple.

Facing up to the facts and reality of violent crime in the Bog, rather than running away and retreating from the truth(by glossing over true racial statistics!), means first facing up to the facts and reality of the true **CULPRITS** of violent crime in the Bog—regardless of race or ethnicity: those childishly contentious and combative belligerents whose natural penchants for violence and vulgarity typically take over once their ever so limited mentality and reason fail so miserably!

Point **IS**, bitter Bog-Bug babies: **STOP** babbling, blabbering, blubbering, clamoring, rambling, harping and running **ON** in extenso **TALKING** racial justice, fairness and equality to frickin' death!

Just **DO IT!!!**

And if contemporary black folk really want to collect those long-overdue *race*-based **REPARATIONS** for the historical atrocities of slavery(which they never suffered) then perhaps they'd take it out in trade for all the **RESTITUTION** owed directly and more immediately to the existing *victims*(alive or dead)of all that rampant **VIOLENT CRIME** blacks are committing so frequently and so indiscriminately all over the place!

"He(David Horowitz)made this claim('that contemporary claims for reparations for slavery are not actually based on any real injury')in a full-page advertisement in UC Berkeley's student-run newspaper on the last day of Black History Month this year," editorialized UC Berkeley associate professor of education, Jabari Mahiri in a column arguing for reparations. "...Black students at the University of California stormed the offices of the newspaper and demanded a public apology, which they later received from the editors."

Craven cowards at the **Daily Cull** should've never apologized for running a legitimate paid editorial column. Free speech and its free exercise never needs nor demands any apology. No part of our constitutional safeguards guarantees *anyone* of *any* race *any* guarantee against ever being *"offended"* in this country of supposed free speech and free expression.

Nor should free speech and its exercise in any sup-

posedly free country ever be subject to the bullying in-
timidation, scare-tactics and suppression of terroristic
gangs of whatever stripe or color.

And the Berkeley **BASHER** directly dares and de-
fies you with *this* challenge: just **TRY** bullying, intimi-
dating, terrorizing or otherwise threatening *him*—much
less demanding any apologies—for freely exercising *his*
constitutional(and human)rights of free speech and
free expression and just see how far you get!

Why is it then, really, that bitter Bog-Bugs think so
misguidedly and self-deludedly that the backward, barbaric, butt-*ugly* Bog of Berkeley is the sole hideout for
so-called *"diverse"* peoples on the entire frickin' planet??? Can anyone, anywhere say?

Let's get this straight once and for all frickin' time:
some obscure ethnic or racial coloring of skin does
NOT—NOT, I say!—"diversity" make!

So just stop deluding and kidding yourselves, bitter
Bog-Bugs! No two people living, breathing and walking our commonly shared earth are exactly alike! Everyone, everywhere is different, disparate, distinct and
frickin' **DIVERSE!** And they exist and survive anywhere and everywhere you may ever go in the world—
even at the middle-most core of middle America!

So wake up, deal with it and get over it, bitter Bog-
Bugs: your surface skin shade makes you nothing special—not here, not anywhere! People's looks, features,
characters, personalities, temperaments, conduct and
behavior—different, disparate and distinct everywhere!—make them far more *"diverse"* than their superficial skin coloring!

UNSAFE SEX: GETTING AND HAVING LOTS AND LOTS OF IT!!!

"Just because you don't(and don't know how to) get it GOOD don't begrudge those who do!"—the Berkeley BASHER

JOSEPH COVINO JR

For sometime now the **Daily Cull** has reverted exploitatively and sensationally to wasting scads of column space so worthlessly by publishing what any other legitimate, professional and reputable newspaper would call outright **FLUFF:** a frickin' weekly sex-advice column titled *"Sex on Tuesdays."* Yes, the **Daily Cull**—that student-run recycled paper that can't even write in inverted pyramid-style the who–what–when–where–how–and–why of a **HARD NEWS** story much less pick put a value-laden news peg to base it on!

As one correspondent wrote in to the paper about its weekly sex-advice column silliness: "There is many a better place to get the information, not to mention a better context."

INDEED!

After all, what can some little snotnosed, wet–behind–the–ears punk **KID** barely out of her frickin' dirty diapers teach **ANY** of us about lovemaking much less sex in spite of her imperious and impertinent injunctions to curious readers to write to ask **HER** questions so they might "learn" from **HER** a thing or two about **SEX???!!!**

And one of the things one of the little girls writing the **Daily Cull's** weekly "sexpert" sex-advice column sometime ago most presumptuously spread all abroad, like some rampantly contagious sexually transmitted disease, was what **SHE** misguidedly thought was some "great saying." Sex, she heard, "is perfectly natural, but rarely is it naturally perfect."

Well, speak for your frickin' selves, little **kiddies!**

Following the fashion of such sage and profound sexual saws of wisdom it's no wonder that all such self-styled sex columnists do nothing but perpetuate mass psychosexual neuroses and perfectly artificial, contrived, self-conscious, labored and ***UNNATURAL*** sexual acts and practices!

And if you honestly doubt just how deeply and psycho-sexually neurotic Americans really are about sex just go to the movies and pay close attention to audience reaction to so-called "graphic" love or sex scenes.

Watch closely how captive movie-goers squirm uncomfortably in their theater seats as they're forced to watch awkward actors make not only love but ***LAME*** and ***LOUSY*** love on the big silver screen—especially those adolescent acting graduates of the very same voracious, ***CAMEL***–smacking–and–sucking school of gaping-mouthed French kissing!

Or during more dated movies just listen to those puerile groupies from Film 101 class—intensely indoctrinated by pop culture to be witless voyeurs—cackle childishly when scenes of imminent sexual suspense fade to black, depriving them of the exceptionally cheap thrill of their expected film fix of insipid soft porn!

I ***MEAN:*** do any among those hordes of juvenile movie-goers still lining up after all these years to see *Last Tango In Paris* honestly find that excruciatingly ***TORTUROUS*** scene of a lumbering Marlon Brando, heaving and humping upright against that little French girl banged up against the wall—like some buffalo bull in heat from *Golden Gate Park* in San Francisco—sexually ***EROTIC???!!!***

Resorting more to their how-to sex manuals and guidebooks than to real-life, real-world knowledge and experience self-deluded "sexpert" columnists prove to be obsessively preoccupied more with ***MECHANICAL*** sexual methods, techniques, props and trappings than with real lovemaking or true intimacy since they're invariably inexperienced(or inept)at making real love—if not utterly ignorant of that delicate distinction between lovemaking and what they so euphemistically refer to as "having sex."

Straining so stiffly and so tensely with some sexual *"partner"* to push all the right sexual buttons, pull all the right sexual levers and flip all the right sexual switches is supposed to be sexually *"creative,"* you see. And *"casual"* sex is something you're supposed to relish only with strangers while lovemaking is reserved solely for lovers!—as if lovers aren't ever supposed to have any downright bawdy and raunchy **SEX!!!** Think **AGAIN**, little kiddies!!!

So if you really want to learn mechanical and machine-like sex and lovemaking then by all means: take and follow the so-called "advice" of those published "sexpert" hacks and mechanics! Trying to learn lovemaking or even sex from them is much like ineffectual children trying to learn about life and living from other equally ineffectual children—earning learning results that must necessarily prove to be faulty and inferior!

People of mature sexual awareness, knowledge and experience already know full well that the most nearly perfect lovemaking or sex is that which happens freely, naturally and spontaneously between impassioned lovers in intimate relationships and which, in turn, comes out of their intensest and innermost desires, feelings and emotions.

Such passions are simple, pure and free of artificial or mechanical contrivance. Such passions come deeply and profoundly from **WITHIN** rather than so artificially or superficially from without. In a few words: such passions are **UNFORCED!**

If these passions fail to freely, naturally and spontaneously catch fire well before lovemaking or sex even begins then all the artificially contrived sexual aids, devices, advice and mechanical methods—and childish

WISHFUL THINKING—in the whole wide world will fail miserably to impassion the soul much less arouse its desire!

Doubtless many of you out there, having and reveling in your truly intimate and latex-**LESS** lovemaking and sex, must be utterly **SICK** and **TIRED** of the **Daily Cull** "sexpert" preaching perpetually to abstain from the consummate joy of exchanging and sharing "body-fluids!"

Misery loves company, we know, but so much precious column space is wasted so worthlessly by rehashing the very same tired, tedious and bombastic soapbox sermons of someone getting **NONE**—and then forcing them on those among the rest of us getting and enjoying the whole glorious she**BANG** as it were!

HOT is, after all, better than **NOT!**

And if it's honestly still so "difficult for people to talk about sex," as some pseudo-"sexpert" was quoted by the Daily **Cull** as harping so habitually on that tired and tedious safe–sex–as–terror–tactics theme then these sexual cripples masquerading as sexperts have **MADE** not only talking about it but actually **DOING** it so absurdly, so asininely, so foolishly, so inanely, so ludicrously, so preposterously, so ridiculously, so senselessly, so stupidly, so **LABORIOUSLY DIFFICULT**— and the weekly sex-advice column so worthlessly a **WASTE** of precious column space!

As that past correspondent so astutely advised: "Come on, *Daily Cal*...deal with it yourselves!"

Now let's get down to the dirty nitty-gritty of the **shitty** sex the **Daily Cull's** supposed sexperts so *in*expertly propagate.

These completely clue-**LESS** chicks—typically homely and runty little girls invariably named Chin, Chan, Chang, Chung, Jung or something akin to

"Itches"(which makes you wonder what *she's* infected with!)—really haven't even the remotest idea or notion of what **real** sex really is!

According to these poor, pathetic, misguided crybabies **SEX**—as they're so fond of repeating so redundantly ad nauseam ad infinitum—is *"anything* or whatever you(and sometimes a mutually consenting partner)want it to be!" So **THERE!** *Nyah, Nyah, Nyah, Nyah!!!!*

Well, I hate to so sadly disillusion you little kiddies, but no, sex is most absolutely, definitely and positively **NOT** just "anything" you want it to be! That's severely adolescent and childish **WISHFUL THINKING**—*not* sex!

Oh, sure, you can dream, fabricate, fantasize, invent, wish and insist that anything's whatever you want it to be all you want but that won't ever necessarily make it so—at least not in any actual realm of reality except that of your own warped whimsy or distorted dreamland.

You can leap off that 307-foot **Campanile** clock(**Sather**)tower on Cal campus and insist all you want—until Doomsday!—that once you hit bottom you'll harmlessly bounce off(rather than splatter all over)the hard and unyielding pavement below like a buoyant and springy trampoline. But it won't happen.

You can even insist on rudely jay-walking at the Bog's deadliest intersection at Shattuck and University Avenues and wish all you want—likewise until Doomsday!(most likely yours!)—that when that careening two-ton vehicle finally slams into you its solid steel bumper will buckle and you'll walk away utterly unscathed(and your scrawny-ass frame won't really be flattened all over the asphalt!). That won't happen either.

Nor is the essential and irreducible sum and substance of **SEX**—sexual **INTERCOURSE**(male penile penetration of the female vagina)—likely to change the grim reality just to suit your infantile fantasies and wishful thinking!

As the old saying goes, sex is first for *procreation*—not recreation. So like it or not little kiddies: if the chick penetrated can't potentially get pregnant by it, *IT* ain't sex—*PERIOD!*

Anything and everything else in the realm of sexual actions, activity, conduct and behavior comprises sexual acts or practices—but never, *ever* sex *PER SE!* It takes both Xs and Ys to impregnate and proliferate! That's why the entire perverted concept of "gay marriage" is so absurdly silly and ridiculous! Two Xs or two Ys ain't gonna knock up let alone fertilize *ANYTHING*—no matter how much infantile wishful thinking is indulged in! An X without a Y just don't—and won't—cut it! Never has, never will! Not now, not ever! *You can't impossibly marry what you can't possibly consummate!* Got that? Good!

But then again since sex is supposed to be "anything *whatever* you want" then maybe *BESTIALITY* could become the latest fad and all the rage for those deliberately self-deluded *Daily Cull* "sexpert" columnists! Like, I thought I saw a *putty-cat!* Like, I thought I saw a *HOT* putty-cat!

Now that we've most effectively re-established and reminded ourselves what *real* sex actually and truly *is* let's clue these deliberately self-deluded dreamers, fantasizers and wishful thinkers in and put them wise about what sex is *NOT!* Sex most absolutely, definitely and positively *isn't:*

•**Condoms.** If you're resorting to condoms don't ever kid yourself: you're not getting properly laid or having proper sex! Latex-separated private parts and displaced bodily fluids and sex juices comprises neither intimacy nor sex!

•**Lube Job.** If you've got to oil or otherwise grease up the appropriate sexual organs or orifices with lame-ass lubricants to get laid by the opposite sex then one or the other of you *LOSERS*—or both—are either malfunctioning(dessicated and dried-up)units or unstimulating(or unstimulated)participants!

•**Masturbation**. Abusing yourself is better and preferred to abusing non-human animals, I suppose, but it's still a *sorry-ass substitute* for *LOSERS* not getting a steady diet of getting laid by the opposite sex! Solo sex is supposedly the safest sex: yeah, well, so is *celibacy*—of which masturbation is just a sorry-ass *off-shoot!* So if all you can get to do is masturbate then you might just as well stay *abstinent*; for there's just no two ways about it: gettin' *off* by itself just ain't the same satisfying thing without gettin' *IN* first! You could say that the Daily *Cull*-propagated style of "sex" amounted to *mutual* masturbation!

•**Sex Toys.** Sex toys, so-called, are either sorry-assed substitutes for *LOSERS* having *non-existent* sex or lame-assed excuses for *LOSERS* having *shitty* sex! Your call which but no matter how you slice it: *play*things ain't ever the **real** things! The exact same goes for resorting to clamps, clips, dental dams, lollies, strap-ons and *Saran wrap* of all things! If you're wrapping it up in cellophane you might as well just give it up and hang it up! *Plastic* sex never amounts to anything resembling really **hot–wet–and–wild** sex! Nor does Inquisitional torture devices wielded by some latter-day *Torquemada!*

•**Body Piercings.** As for painfully(and stupidly)piercing with infection-inviting bits of metal intimate and private parts of your body(like genitalia, nipples, tongue), much less other parts like the chin, ears, navel, nose or wherever, that **bestiality** thing again comes into play—with *domesticated farm animals* coming to mind—which plausibly explains why so many if not most of these perforated chumps look as well as act so **bestial! FARMS** in *Berkeley???!!!*

GAWD! It's no wonder sexual dysfunction, so-called, is reputedly so rampant among the present-day punk population! They've replaced all their natural bodily functions and creative imaginations with assorted(and sordid)artificial props and cheap trappings! What's worse, they've reduced the fine art and artistry of sex to the "guided" instructions of hack mechanics whereby sexual givers and receivers take turns giving and taking robotic–"erotic" directions while articulating supposedly constructive little critiques of one another's techniques(for purposes of "communication")along the way! **BOR-ING!!!** Your dogs could do better tricks and doubtless do! And if that's how you're really going about getting down and getting it on then I feel very, **VERY** sorry for you! As one **Daily Cull** "sexpert" so pompously put it, it sucks to be **YOU!**

Now let's get **REAL** here(as you punks are so fond of admonishing others)and face some simple *facts of life*:

SEX is mostly about a *mutual sharing* of *sensual sensations* intensified most profoundly by the *passion* of *emotional* and *erotic* if not *loving feelings*.

You don't *talk* sex—you **feel** and **sense** sex! You don't *direct* sex—you **DO** sex—**TOGETHER**—pure and simple! And no, it doesn't take clairvoyance, extrasensory perception or even psychic ability as some "sexpert" columnists so sarcastically suggest. It simply takes some acutely conscious *sensual sensitivity* and some *creative imagination* conjured up along the way! So long as you're fixated on your silly little directions and critiques, so long as you're obsessing over your equally silly little props and trappings it's no wonder you're not getting off as *intensely HOT* as you should be!

Concentrate instead then on *mutually feeling* and *sensing* sex as you go at it—and *each other—together* with *mutual lust* if not *love!* That means quite simply resorting to your **carnal senses**—not your torturous-ly *TEDIOUS diarrhetic diatribes of the motormouth!* He gives it, she gives it up and you both get off together. If you can't do that then just shut up, admit you're a brain-dead air-head and *MOVE ON* to your next dorky dick-head or dumb-fuck!

That scarcely means that some honestly salacious and seductive speech can't be effectively thrown into the sexual mix. But *please, really, come ON*...blah, blah, blah: if you and your mutually consenting lov-er can't simply *LOCK LIPS AND LOINS, HUMP, JUMP* and *PUMP* and *BURN UP THE BED*(or other location)then you're more than likely with the wrong "partner" to start with—and all the artificial(and unnatural)sexual aids, props and trappings in all the world will do neither of you *jack-shit* in getting you some honestly *HOT* ass or action!

Exploit and make the most of what the **Good Lord** and the **Grand Design** *naturally* gave you! If you don't believe in either(or anything else beyond your paltry self)—and still labor under the misguided delu-sion that you're *so* special and the center of the known universe around which everything else supposedly re-volves—then stop flattering yourself and get over your-self: or the next time you want to make a *real* kid to-gether *naturally*(without the *artificial manipulation* of reproductive material in a test tube!)then just try to *beget* and get with child on your own(alone)with any of your array of ineffectual and sterile sexual aids or toys! Then you'll finally realize by yourself just how *insignificant* and outright *pathetic* you really are!

Anything else—like most *everything* else in the backward, barbaric, butt-**UGLY** Bog of Berkeley—is sheer superfluous **PRETENSION!**

Whatever, *screw **SHITTY SEX!***

Now take none of this wrong, little kiddies. I'm a "traditional" live–and–let–live liberal from and of the old classical school, and as such I couldn't give a *flying hang* how you go your own way or how freaky, geeky or kinky you get—whether you're straight, gay, lesbian, bisexual, transsexual or even trans-**SPECIES**(in the event of you naturally *bestiality*–gender–oriented–sexual–preferenced adherents out there! After all, sex can be anything you damn well please, right?! So there! Nyah, nyah!!)—just stop **BORING** everybody to **TEARS** by trying so futilely to foist upon the entire planet your artificial, perverted and unnatural acts and practices by palming them off as "sex" and "marriage." They're neither so get over **IT** and **YOURSELVES** at one fell swoop!

Nobody has to either like or "accept" you. Nobody likely even gives a rap in the first frickin' place! Just stop trying to manipulate, redefine and tamper with "sex" and "marriage" by attempting so impossibly to *compel* what's natural and normal to *conform* to what's abnormal, artificial and unnatural! In short, stop grand-standing and putting on the ever so conspicuously *self-conscious* front by trying so ineptly to pass off what's **FAKE** and **PHONY** for what's **REAL** and **TRUE!**

You're kidding nobody but yourselves and nothing but age, maturity or *decline* will effectively—and beneficially—cure you. And believe me, the cure *will* ultimately come. But in the meantime nobody's buying *it*—or *you.* So sell it to the ***GULLIBLE!*** And save your petty name-calling misnomers(like "hetero*sexist*")for the ***SUPERSTITIOUS!***

STRAIGHT MALE CHAUVINIST PIG TALK FOR THE GUYS ONLY

L et me pose some open questions to you:
•Did you choose and come to university in desperate search of preachy, surrogate parents disguised as "sexpert" columnists telling you how to live and enjoy your rightfully private sex life?

•Do you gullibly buy into the mostly truthless terror tactics about sexually transmitted diseases*(STDs,* so-called)that pander to and play into the profiteering hands of pseudo-scientific researchers and pharmaceutical drug companies—not to mention ***CONDOM-*** makers?

•Are you at all sick and tired of bitchy, squealing, puppet-ically correct California chicks ***TALKING*** sex to frickin' death rather than ***DOING*** and ***FEELING*** and ***SENSING*** sex by trying to ***DIRECT*** your each and every move under the deceptive pretense of "pleasing your partner?"

•Are you at all sick and tired of being called "sexist" simply because you refuse to use condoms for having "safe" and **FAKE** sex?

•Are you at all sick and tired of "sexpert" columnists trying to thrust down your deep throat their silly and stupid notions of what "successful sex" is supposed to be?

•Don't you mightily wish that those very same "sexpert" columnists would just stay in their own frickin' bedroom and **OUT** of yours—giving your most intimate and sacred sex life at least some **SEMBLANCE** of privacy and respect???

If so then **HAVE NO FEAR**—the Berkeley **BASHER's** here to offer you some tangible and most puppetically **INCORRECT** tips on that all-important topic: **SEX!!!**

Now I've been most blest and fortunate to have seduced my exceptional share of beautiful, consenting, warmly willing and sumptuously voluptuous(I **DO** *love* them fleshy and fuller-figured—as in busty and lusty!)over my blessedly long and lustful sex life but I've never resorted to raping any woman—nor would I ever want to or even try!

But—now hear this loud and clear and mark me well: nor have I ever nor would I ever use a frickin' **CONDOM**. And nor do you **HAVE** to!

Like what I just wrote or not—and I could really give a frick **LESS** either way!—listen up, little kiddies, and check this out closely: the very **DEEP DIFFERENCE** between me and those puppet-ically correct proselytizers is that I'm honestly **NOT** trying to convert **ANYONE** to my own personal point of view on the question at issue(condom use)by telling anyone else—very **UNLIKE** them!—what they **SHOULD** or **OUGHT TO** do in their own private sex lives much less how they should get their rocks off! Got **THAT? GOOD!**

So I'll come straight and swiftly to the point: *pass*

up those mostly frustrated, neurotic and puppet-ically correct California chicks and ***ETHNIC***–Assimilated–American women for making love or having sex!

Shower both your attention and affection instead on the truly ethnic women of the "fairer sex" visiting the Bog from other countries in faraway lands! Yes, I mean truly ***FOREIGN*** women in the truest ***FOREIGNER*** sense!

If you've got a hang-up or ***PROBLEM*** with that parlance then by all means go bluster all about your semantic resentments to the ego-endangered "editors" at the ***Daily Cull*** where they'll really get ***OFF*** on them!

Why then would I offer you this invaluable but unsolicited advice?

Well, admittedly generalizing from my own first-hand personal experience: foreign women are far more sensual and genuinely sexually liberated than American women mostly because they're quite unashamed to remain sweetly feminine and actually revel in their womanly and unabashedly ***UN***-manly differences from men—meaning they aren't senselessly trying to be "one of the boys!" So no whimsically wishful thinking there!

They carry next to no feminist, sex-phobic baggage or paranoia when they visit so they play no head games with men and come with no sexually-evangelical missions to carry on and no sexually-domineering points or put-downs to make!

Best of all: if they like you enough to ***BONK*** you then they let you know it directly and straight-forward-ly without any adolescent, brain-teasing, body-taunting ***ANTICS!***

And best of all beyond that: they luxuriate in true ***INTIMACY***, meaning they also take ***FULL RESPON-SIBILITY*** for their ***OWN BODIES***(their ***OWN***

SELVES)when they make their own free, willing and consenting choice to spread and open up their desirous and desirable legs to a condom-*LESS* male whom they will do as *THEY* please to sleep with—all *WITHOUT* expecting *YOU* to bear that *RESPONSIBILITY* rightfully and totally belonging to them *ALONE! THANK YOU VERY MUCH!!!*(Any of you over-presumptuous chicks out there expecting guys you're letting screw you to first ask your "permission" before ejaculating inside your wussy-pussies need to just keep your slutty thighs snugly *SHUT* in the first frickin' place!).

These foreigners are *REAL* women who still appreciate and savor the simple but sublime beauty of a chivalrous compliment, a knowing and meaningful glance, a tender and loving exchange of sentiments, a soft and warm caress of cheeks, a gentle and lingering touch of lips, a deep and profound embrace!

Over and above all that they're mostly possessed of a certain articulate, eloquent and *INTELLIGENT* command of language and faculty of speech(for carrying on a coherent conversation!)far exceeding the typical California chick's 91/2–word vocabulary: *Awesome! Bummer! Cool! Great! Omigod! Totally! Yeah, right! Like, WHATEVER!*

And they'd never, ever even *DARE* to ruin or spoil a rapturously passionate and romantic moment much less cheapen and demean the reverent intimacy of real love-making by demanding that you cover your cod with a condom!

Sorry, little kiddies, but *NO WAY*: copulating with a sex-segregating condom is, strictly speaking, neither love-making nor sex!

So don't be at all put off by snotty wisecracks made by snooty but self-flattering California chicks who, sorely confusing snarling surliness for "strength"—and who typically act superior way beyond their actual appeal—smack of the **SAPPY!**

And don't panic and act so desperate either: if she does demand a condom and you're adamantly against it(as I am)then politely but firmly proclaim that it's against your conviction(or religion or "whatever")and just as politely but promptly *excuse* yourself, get up and zip up to **walk!** I guarantee you: if they're truly *hot to trot* enough to get *it*(and you)then they'll both give *in* and give *it up*—as they invariably do or else they wouldn't be in that not–so–compromising position in the first frickin' place!

So go for the **REAL DEAL**, guys—whether African, Asian, European, Latina or "whatever": they'll not only want **IT** and give themselves up to **IT** but they'll literally feast and thrive on taking **IT**—and **YOU!!!**

TRUST ME ON THIS ONE!!!

Footnote: forgive the coarse, crass and crude parlance of this chapter but it was deemed necessary to **"dumb down"** for the benefit of uncouth **Daily Cull** columnists and editors.

JOSEPH COVINO JR

PROFESSION OF FAITH: SHOW RESPECT IF NOT REVERENCE

For the longest time the **Daily Cull** used to periodically publish painter Warner Sallman's famed iconic *Head of Christ(1940)*, which someone or some group of faith paid to print along with captioned biblical quotes. Beneath the portrait the ignorant **Daily Cull** would regularly run the irreverently disparaging and disrespectful disclaimer to spinelessly distance itself from even the remotest hint or implication of any religious or spiritual affiliation: *PAID ADVERTISEMENT!*

These inexcusable, indefensible episodes not only insulted the discerning intelligence of the recycled paper's astute readers—as if they couldn't frickin' figure out for themselves that the picture and caption were religiously separate, apart and dis-associated with the recycled paper's puppet-ically correct athiestic agenda—but also degraded and demeaned the most sacred, solemn and spiritual beliefs of the truest and most devout believers by falsely insinuating that faith is some thing put up for sale for profit or gain!

Now no one **HAS** to believe in God or Jesus Christ but anyone should at least have the good taste, good manners, common courtesy and simple decency to at least show true and devout believers some ***SEM-BLANCE*** of civilized respect and consideration!

To set right this petty and piddling(*faith-phobic and religious-istic*)prejudice against people of faith and their religious and spiritual beliefs I'll get out here the once censored answer I gave to an athiestic column put out by one of the recycled paper's bigoted writers whose unworthy name won't be worth mentioning:

If the God I know and believe in was ever as insolent and infantile in attitude as the *Daily Cull* columnist was about things sacred and spiritual, grappling with the open question—*"Is God Worth It?"*—then I'm very sure God Himself could very well ask: is the canting *Daily Cull* columnist worth it???

But as many of us already know full well God is neither vindictive nor unforgiving: He loves everyone equally—doubters, skeptics and sinners alike! So if only I could be as persevering as the *Daily Cull* columnist in my own conviction that if enough people simply ignored the ignorance of foolish people they too would somehow just *"go away."*

That *Daily Cull* columnist disparagingly belittles and ridicules "religious" people as being "talking heads" having none of the keen logic and acute rationality he so very misguidedly ***THINKS*** and ***PRETENDS*** he has. He says he feels sorry for those he thinks "lost themselves to their religious beliefs" by letting their religion take "control of their lives."

What exactly is the *Daily Cull* columnist together with the likes of his "clear-thinking" circle lost to and controlled by? Arrogance? Cynicism? Incivility? Irreverence? Secularism? Profanity? Vanity? Vulgarity? Immorality? Immaturity? ***INHUMANITY???*** Traits as "marvelous" as the *Daily Cull* columnist's supposed "truth."

Perhaps these more so than established religion as such are "overblown" notions to which "far too many lives are lost"—including the *Daily Cull* columnist's! Perhaps we should all "feel sorry" for the *Daily Cull* columnist as he might well feel sorry for himself since *mis*-using or *un*-using your own mind is the worst and most tragic "waste" of all!

"To believe so strongly in something that constantly proves itself to be wrong is not my idea of a sound investment," the **Daily Cull** columnist prosyletized.

But if he'd only carry his own irrationality and endlessly faulty assumptions to their very illogical conclusions then he'd prove himself as soundly wrong as his presumptuous, know–it–all self-investiture is **UN**-sound! So if anything "feeds on ignorance" it's ignorance itself more than religion as such.

Faith is hardly the means of understanding the meaning and purpose of human earthly existence or even of explaining the un-explainable "questions of the universe" or of appeasing anyone's petty curiosity about the "meaning of life and death."

People of faith already know and understand the true meaning and purpose of human earthly existence, having as it does absolutely nothing whatever to do with attaching any importance to God as being "responsible for worldly acts" by means of "divine intervention."

The faithful already know that God is the First Cause, Creator and Source of all things, including the **Daily Cull** columnist's own very limited and earthbound mentality—out of which such things were mentioned as: plate tectonics, human fertilization, thunderbolt-hurling clouds!

As Jesus Christ Himself said: *"The wind blows where it wills, and you can hear the sound it makes, but you do not know where it comes from or where it goes. And so it is with everyone who is born of the Spirit."*

Lay the blame for exploiting religion as a pretext for killing people and waging unholy wars where it rightfully belongs: not on God or faith but on the belligerent, bloodthirsty and murderous materialists, rationalists and so-called "free-thinkers" distorting and perverting faith so maliciously to suit their own self-serving ends and purposes.

Work your God-given brain just a teeny-weenie bit and **THINK**, Mr. **Daily Cull** columnist, **THINK!**

How much horrific but strictly sectarian strife having absolutely nothing whatever to do with religion as such goes on day after bloody day the world over? How many countless human lives have been lost over the ages to the secular "science" of military arms, armament and warfare? Scientific and secular hardly always equate with ethical and moral, do they???

Open up your muddled and mundane mind, Mr. **Daily Cull** columnist and take a good, clear-headed and honest look all around you: can a truly sensing man explain only what he's actually experienced? Have you never yet felt the utter joy of feeling a woman's very soul from having intense and loving intimacy with her? My God, man, how and where have you spent your time for almost a quarter of a century???

Why, all life and creation are heavenly and divine! If you're so special and superior, Mr. **Daily Cull** columnist, could you yourself possibly recreate or reproduce even a single infinitesimal iota of it? And the Source of the universe is the very Incarnation of the infinite and eternal mystery keeping the universe in perfect working order—causing and creating it from the very beginning!

Jesus Christ was most assuredly right when He said that many people's hearts were so hardened that they may look and hear but they never really see much less listen or understand. And when one blind person guides or leads another both eventually fall into a pit!

Faith is hardly about "preparing for death." Rather,

it's about preparing for *LIFE*—in both the here and now as well as the hereafter. And like hope and love faith is a virtue which is best *PRACTICED* rather than proved by virtuous thought, word and deed—much like the *Daily Cull* columnist's own mother trying so fruitlessly to persuade her ungrateful son to pray!

And like those other virtues faith needs no proof. Divinity and heavenliness in all life and creation are their own sole proof.

Why? Very simple really: because neither science nor secularism can ever, nor will they ever, *RE*-create life or creation in all their profound perfection and wonder as perfectly and wondrously—miraculously, if you will—as they've already been created!

Believe it or not, as unbelievable as it may seem or sound to you, God is an act much too hard for even any *Daily Cull* columnist to follow! After all, a *Daily Cull* columnist and his words will most definitely pass away(and ever so swiftly!)—along with heaven and earth!—but God's Word will *NEVER* pass away!

If you still remain unconvinced, Mr. *Daily Cull* columnist, just ask yourself: how many countless generations of the world have with truth passed away since God's Word was first spoken on this earth? *Really*, will any words of *yours* last even nearly as long?

If you really want to prove(scientifically speaking of course!)to everyone just how totally "self-sufficient" and free of God's creative control you really are, Mr. *Daily Cull* columnist, simply try for all of us this telling empirical experiment: totally deprive yourself of divine creation's air and water—thoroughly polluted by faulty and unsound *HUMAN* science no less!—and all the science, technology and e-mailgrams of sympathy in the known human universe will never, ever save you!

Where's the "benefit" in having faith you ask, Mr. **Daily Cull** columnist? In truly using the human mind God gave you. In truly **THINKING** and following your own advice: doing—perhaps even **WRITING**—something, **ANYTHING** *"productive!"*

You **DO** realize you have a *free will*, don't you? But can you prove absolutely by your own all-powerful "science" beyond any and all doubt that it's actually there—or where it came from?

Know and understand that your God-given human intellect and reason, wherever you may think or believe these come from—obviously **NOT** from the **BIG BANG** in your special case, Mr. **Daily Cull** columnist!—are yours to use as you please and will for good or for ill. And the only proof you'll ever need of these being heavenly or divine is believing and knowing that how **EVER** you may use them is in essence the God-given gift of *free choice!*

You may very well *program* your extremely scientific and technical computer to choose as freely as you do. But neither you nor *it* will ever, ever *cause or create* choice—let alone that intangible but vital *life force*(the God-given human soul)that sparks *conscious awareness* in even the most **MINUSCULE** of human minds!

POLITICS

Politics we can dismiss simply this way:

Politics is neither the "art of compromise" nor the "struggle for power" over people's minds and actions as some highfalutin political "thinkers" have so superficially supposed.

Politics is, rather, the art(or rather *artifice*)of convenience and expedience as well as the struggle for the freedom and independence of action to do and **GET AWAY** and **GET OFF** scot-free with doing whatever is most convenient and expedient—**NOT** whatever is most humanly beneficial, ethical, fair, good, just, moral, right or virtuous!

Compromise and power may either or both be mere **MEANS** of gaining those very same self-serving ends of political convenience, expedience, freedom and independence of action!

EPILOGUE: MOVIE MANIA, THE ENGLISH PATIENT'S MISSING LOVE-QUOTIENT, AND JOY-LUCK CLUBBED!

*"**Even** Fantasy Studios, **which produced films such as** Amadeus **and** The English Patient, **chose Berkeley over Hollywood.**"*—City•*Stupid* Guide

JOSEPH COVINO JR

Their faces are thoroughly timeworn—older, graying, wrinkled with age—and would likely appear to some to be anything but star-gazingly cinematic. Their dramatic backdrop has spanned the farm land of northern California and the Oakland hills rather than the more suggestively exotic and panoramic locales of Italy and Tunisia. And their own very personal love story will likely never catapult them to the momentarily fashionable fame of those illicit, star-crossed lovers(Katherine and Count Laszlo de Almasy)cavorting so shamelessly and unscrupulously in that latterly but overly-hyped and artificially contrived silver screen romance so graphically and luridly played out in that most pretentious of major motion picture wanna-be–but–flopped film epics: ***The English Patient(EP)!***

But surely the deep and devoted love that these two venerable lovers have known and shared for almost five decades far outshines—in both utter truth and purity—the sordid, lust-driven pretense and perversion of love so surreptitiously portrayed in the *EP*.

These days you might very well find these two love-birds—Darby and Joan we'll call them for want of their real names since they carefully cherish their privacy—sitting in some fast food restaurant or coffee shop, quietly eating, talking or simply relaxing, her head typically resting on his shoulder as if he were the softest and most buoyant of pillows. And in spite of being looked down on by the witlessly puppet-ically correct police they prefer to see themselves not as "partners" but as an unabashed ***COUPLE***—and clearly a loving one at that!

Could this inseparably wedded pair be considered some charmed aberration? After all, by their own account they're the sole couple taking thrifty lunches together at a neighborhood senior center. And at first sight they might even appear destitute and homeless: even in the mid-80s I recall seeing them scavenging the streets late at night for stacks of discarded newspapers to recycle for cash.

So why set off these two gentle old souls against the leading man and woman of a popular, oscar-winning major motion picture? Because: by their lasting love and lifelong loyalty to each other they personify true **TOGETHERNESS.**

Beyond faithlessness and passing physical passion what else could recommend Katherine and the Count to anyone as lovers of unfailing value and worth? One movie critic reviewing the *EP*—an insidiously corrupt story that essentially begins with marital infidelity and ends with murderous euthanasia—called it a "celebration of betrayal." Far worse, it's a **GLORIFICATION** of it!

No doubt the *EP* will be the Berkeley Bog's most self-congratulating **SACRED COW** for some years to come—artificially immune to uncensored, plain-spoken, published criticism. And granted it's a well-acted, well-mounted if poorly photographed film boasting colorful locales, picturesque landscapes and grandiose music. But contrary to mindlessly widespread wishful thinking the *EP* is most assuredly no movie epic on an equal par with **Lawrence of Arabia** or **Dr. Zhivago**—to which certain self-deluding, self-flattering circles have misguidedly compared it!

So it's scarcely surprising that the *EP's* production studio would've chosen to base itself in the *capital of artificial contrivance and pretention:* the **Bog!** If nothing else we can very precisely predict: the *EP* will be celebrating no silver or golden anniversary revivals—fated only to be dumped rapidly into the great dustbin of obliviously forgotten films substituting trappings of style for substance!

Life and lot permitting on the other hand Darby and Joan will doubtless celebrate their 50-year golden marriage anniversary if they haven't already by this time. Very much unlike Katherine and the Count their love is deeply and irrevocably rooted not in betrayal but in constant and unbroken **TRUST**. Trust lies first and last at the very heart and soul of this couple's most critical "core belief."

"Trust is the most basic thing," Joan will tell you most emphatically and unequivocally. "I couldn't live without that. If you can't believe in someone how can you exist?"

Darby and Joan have both lived and endured together by sharing together—in **TRUST**—everything in a modern world in which staying together, they say, tragically has "less value." Darby sums up their shared togetherness quite simply as "living with integrity."

Darby and Joan are second generation Japanese Americans(*Nisei*)from early 20th-century immigrant families. Their faith lies in Buddhism. Their love lies in living together. Their hope lies in surviving together.

Over their many years of living and surviving together Darby and Joan have worked long and hard, made and lost money, bore and bred a family, raising two sons. And during World War II they were both separately made "*prisoners–of–war*" in the country of their birth afflicted at the time with an epidemic paranoia induced by mostly imaginary saboteurs, spies, subversives and enemy aliens from within—happening to have as well Japanese faces.

So in their youthful prime of life Darby and Joan were each forcibly uprooted from their families and moved separately by the *U.S. War Relocation*

*Authority(WRA)*to those notoriously harsh wartime internment camps—and which in their cases the equivalent of farm stables Darby unhesitatingly calls "concentration camps."

"They destroyed our families and ruined our lives," Joan recounts sadly.

Darby and Joan first met in northern California through the fraternizing of their rural families. During the war each of their families spent some five years in internment camps. Being younger Darby and Joan were officially allowed to leave their separate camps after some two years—only to be inducted and exploited as cheap laborers to help re-stock the nation's shrinking worker supply. Darby considers that he was a two–time–prisoner–of–war after being drafted from his internment camp into the U.S. Army.

Separated some four years by wartime internment and "relocation" Darby and Joan finally reunited—again through the friendship of their families—courted for three years after which they united in marriage. That was in late 1949. They've lived in love—and integrity—ever since. True love and loyalty, at least in their wartime romance saga, are more about the longevity of living and sharing a lifetime together than about fleeting lust.

Now I'm no prude. But I can most definitely attest that there's absolutely nothing whatever glamorous, romantic or even glorious about betrayal and infidelity, especially if you've ever suffered the trenchant pain of it. And only a movie like the *EP*—propagating the warped values of characters acting without *conscience* or *compunction*—would even try so fruitlessly to glamorize, romanticize and glorify it!

Why else would it portray the victimized husband as a perfect **STRAW MAN** of no importance and beneath any sympathy or consideration. Conscience and compunction truly are the traits distinguishing truly epic from shallow and superficial characters! And honorableness of purpose distinguishes epic from empty and totally self-indulgent characters!

So for my money, honey, the truly superior story and **BEST** picture of the proximate period was ***Breaking The Waves***—about a truly loving and devoted wife who by choice freely and willingly defiled her own innocence and purity to save her hopelessly crippled husband from despair and death. At least that film's nurse, contrary to the *EP's*, strove tirelessly to preserve the sanctity and sacredness of life rather than stoically euthanize it!

Fawningly reviewing the *EP* for **Buzz** magazine Anne Beatts took clearly perverse pleasure in quoting a recently divorced girlfriend who characterized the film as some bizarre *litmus test*, saying: "When my ex told me he thought it was boring, I knew I was right in divorcing him. Now I wouldn't date a man who didn't like it. He's obviously not in touch with his feminine side."

No, he's obviously just less in touch with his treacherous side!

Quite a telling if not outright **BIZARRE** case—in—point: some woman of apparent shallow character actually testing her romantic relationships against the shallow characters of a shallow film empty of either depth or character! Doubtless her past husband is far better off divorced from such hollow superficiality!

So for my money, then, the *EP* would've ended far better if the film's pitiless straw man husband hadn't missed **PULVERIZING** the Count Laszlo de Almasy with his careening aeroplane!!!

And we can most accurately foresee the fading fate of the aging "movie stars" of such a film: very much like that of smug and stuck-up young women, mistakenly thinking that they're far too special and superior to fraternize with your common man in the street—curtly spurning the feverish attentions and affections of their most ardent admirers and suitors in their tender **YOUTH** but moanfully mourning and bewailing their most conspicuous absence and loss in their *dried*-up, *used*-up and *washed*-up older **AGE!**

Take heed, little kiddies: find something truly meaningful and purposeful in life—your sassy, self-indulgent youth won't last even nearly as long as you think!

JOY-LUCK CLUBBED!

Which calls to mind that great tradition-bashing, Asian–*Assimilated*–American movie soap opera: **Joy Luck Club**—painfully portraying all that's most perniciously **WRONG** with the warped and twisted puppet-ically correct movement and agenda!

At this film's narrated begining a supposed mother's voice wishes for her daughter that she grow to be "too full to swallow any sorrow." Well, the young Asian chicks making featured appearances in this most artificially **CONTRIVED** film soundly drenched in forced crocodile tears—four of the most chronically carping, habitually harping **WHINERS, MARTYRS, SACRIFICIAL LAMBS** and **VICTIMS** ever to self-immolate on the silver screen!—are far too **FULL** of **THEMSELVES**(not to mention **BULL!**)to swallow any sorrow much **LESS** any of their commonly shared false pride, smugness, vanity, conceit and self-glorification!

Their petty character traits range generally from self-defeatism, self-importance, self-pity, self-satisfaction to outright surliness. And their childishly commanding outcries pierce the ears: **I! I! I! Me! Me! Me! Gimme! Gimme! Gimme!**

Four frickin' little grown-up **BRATS!!!**

And from all their sordid little stories about their empty little lives is supposed to be proved this paltry little point: even members of the Asian–**Assimilated**–American "*model minority*" can come out of screwed-up, dysfunctional families and act as crybabyishly silly, stupid and vulgar as their Caucasian-American counterparts—even if their Caucasian-contaminated experience is aberrantly and abnormally **EXCEPTIONAL** to the usual rule of intelligence, good sense and good taste!

This fanatically wishfully thinking film dares even to malign that far superior Asian-Caucasian romance— **World of Suzie Wong** starring Nancy Kwan—maliciously calling it *"racist!"*

Her Hong Kong prostitute character well aside(Actress Vivian Wu played a *"low class concubine"* in the *Club!*)at least Suzie Wong struggled bravely against all odds to take exceptional care of her "illegitimate" baby.

In the *Club*, to the contrary, three different Chinese "mothers" either abandon or outright kill their babies— for whatever whitewashing excuse or alibi! Another "mother" kills herself, committing suicide.

Like many "hip," modern young women of today, demanding that **MEN** share "responsibility" for conception in their own bodies but denying men **ANY** "responsibility" for abortion in their own bodies—the *Club* women too typically take the easiest and most expedient way out! Talk about double standards!

So given this more truthfully complete context I'll close, leaving it to you to judge and decide whose Chinese characterization is more noble, honorable and virtuous!

AFTERWORD:
CHILLING CONCLUSION

"When the end finally comes, I believe that Berkeley will be the last town in America with the ingrained perversity to hold onto its idea of itself."—Michael Chabon

I f by some miraculous *FLUKE* you've somehow managed to wade this far through this much of the deep, dense, boggy, *Birkenstock BULL* of the backward, barbaric, butt-*UGLY* Bog of Berkeley(which a lady friend of mine calls the *"Land of Entitlement"*)then I honestly hope you've swimmingly avoided becoming part and parcel of those most incoherently *MUMBLING, GRUMBLING* Bog-Bug *LOONS* making up most of the fad-following Bog's mostly pompous, pretentious and psycho-*NEUROTIC* parade—and still managed miraculously to keep your sanity and senses!

And if nothing else I honestly hope that once you do manage to strenuously clamber, climb, crawl up and drag yourself well *OUT* of the ever thick and sloppy *MUCK* of the Bog you'll at least steal away carrying this single, solitary message to send and spread abroad among *ALL* your *SHEEPISHLY* passive, puppet-ically correct chums and cronies: *CHILL!!!*

Our commonly shared world turns egocentrically around *NONE* of you—*NOR* around *ANY* of your semantically self-centered, self-interested, self-righteous *RESENTMENTS!!!*—no matter how fanatical, petty or *ULTRA*-sensitive those might be!!!

Nor will our commonly shared world ever, *EVER* change, reform or otherwise adapt solely to suit *ANY* of your most self-righteously indulgent, indignant and intolerant *RESENTMENTS!!!*

Nor will *ANY* of you *FORCE* our commonly shared world to turn around either you or *ANY* of your selfish *RESENTMENTS* by paternalistically censoring or otherwise stifling and suppressing *FREE SPEECH* and *FREE EXPRESSION* of the *TRUTH*, substituting *IT* with the stale, stilted and sterile *PROPAGANDA*(or pet phrases)most redundantly recycled from the self-inflicted *CONFORMITY* of the obsolete and worth-less puppet-ically correct movement—now or *EVER!!!*

When, oh *WHEN*, will you ever, *EVER* get *IT???!!!*

IF you were truly and progressively *TOLERANT* of *DIVERSITY* as you so falsely *CLAIM* then you *WOULD* among other spankingly *SIMPLE* things— here's my *"TOP TEN" wish-list:*

•Let me *ALONE* to walk freely at least *ONE* frickin' block in the Bog in unmolested *PEACE!*

•Let even *David Horowitz* or *David Irving* freely speak their peace and express themselves freely in un-molested *PEACE.* Drowning out voices that "offend" your petty sensibilities is neither liberty nor tolerance!

•*STOP* telling me and everybody *ELSE* how they should or how they're supposed to act, talk or *LIVE THEIR OWN LIVES!* It's your place *NEITHER TO JUDGE NOR SAY!!!* So if you don't like how oth-ers live their lives then *GET A LIFE*(of your own)and *LEAVE THEM ALONE*(to live their own)!!!

•Stop *WHINING* ever so *PROFUSELY* about what a frickin' *VICTIM* you are and how your defense-less and helpless paltry little *LIFE* is so completely

CONTROLLED and **MANIPULATED** by your superficially **EXTERNAL ENVIRONMENT**—lying trampled and crushed at its uncontrolled **MERCY!!!** Real **"EMPOWERMENT"** is knowing **WHO** you are, confidently and securely within yourself, **WITHOUT** anyone else's approval or acclamation!

•Tolerate ill-ideas, ill-thoughts and even ill-words but repudiate ill-**ACTIONS** and mis-**DEEDS!**

•Try out for a frickin' fresh and refreshing **CHANGE** some truly liberated, free-thinking and **INDEPENDENT THOUGHT** by using your **CREATIVE IMAGINATION** to come up with some **IDEAS** more **ORIGINAL** than "diversity," "progressive" and all your equally silly little ethnic/multi-cultural-**ISMS!!!** In short, get a frickin' **BRAIN!!!**

•Could the Bog consider **RE**-naming its annual September festival and parade—*"How Berkeley Can You Be?"*—to truthfully reflect its true gist and spirit: How **FREAKISHLY IDIOTIC, MORONIC AND RETARDED**(or **Bog-Buggy**)can you be???!!!

•Tell and expose to me the dead **SECRET** of that most profound **MYSTERY** of those so-called information **KIOSK**s installed on Center Street in the so-called "downtown" Bog: just **WHAT IS THERE** exactly in the whole, wide, far–flung–dung world of the Bog to be **INFORMED** about or made known or made acquainted with in the first frickin' place???!!!

•Tell and expose to me the dead **SECRET** of that most profound **MYSTERY** of those blue-shirted, police–cadet–looking *Berkeley Guides*: just **WHAT IS THERE** exactly in the whole, wide, far–flung–dung world of the **BOG** to be **GUIDED TO** anyhow???!!!

•**FINALLY**, if the '80s generation was the *"Me"* generation then the '90s–and–beyond generation must most certainly be not the *"Gen-X"* but more accurately and precisely the **Gen-WV** generation: that is, the **WHINER VICTIM** generation!!!

Now all that contemporary **WHINER VICTIM** generation needs is something of material and momentous **SUBSTANCE** to frickin' whine about!!!

"The Mr. Popularity Award in Berkeley has to go to Martin Luther King, Jr.," spouts the City•*Stupid* guide. "He has a civic center, a park, a street, a swim center, and a junior high school named after him."

Yes, indeed: I myself seek infinite inspiration, comfort, consolation and solace in Martin Luther King Jr.'s famous *"I Have A Dream"* speech each and every time I myself dream and indulge in the **ELATED** and **EC-STATIC** reverie of finally and at long last absconding, escaping, fleeing and finally and **FOREVER** getting **WELL OUT** of and **FAR, FAR AWAY FROM** the backward, barbaric, butt-**UGLY** Bog of Berkeley never, **EVER** to return!!!

And when that divinely and heavenly **BLESSED** day does finally come and I finally do gain my blessed liberty and finally do break out and make my getaway, scot-free and at unfettered liberty, I will break loose **SHRIEKING** with **GIDDY GLEE** at the top of my jubilant and triumphant voice:

FREE AT LAST!
FREE AT LAST!
THANK GOD ALMIGHTY!
I AM FREE AT LAST!!!!!!!!!!!!

FINIS!!!

POSTSCRIPT

BEWARE to *take care* during the so-called "cold–and–flu" season in the germ-ridden, virus-infested Bog to carefully avoid picking up from native Bog-Bugs or otherwise coming down with that most dreaded and debilitating seasonal sickness: the *Berkeley **CRUD!!!***

UNITED WE SQUAT–
The Bog's Patriotic Motto

UNCONDITIONAL
NO–MONEY–BACK GUARANTEE:
If for some sour excuse you're dissatis-
fied with this book then don't even THINK
ABOUT asking for your money back since
ANY claim or demand for ANY REFUND
will be most CHEERFULLY REFUSED!!!

JOSEPH COVINO JR

ABOUT THE WRITER

Joseph Covino Jr is a Florida-bred writer economically imprisoned in ever-whining *Berzerkeley*—the ever-victimized Bog he **LOVES** to **HATE** but would **LOVE** to **ESCAPE** to **EUROPE** even if only as a temporary **FUGITIVE!**

Now that he's given full vent to his most invigorating and healthful **HATE**, having fully **PURGED** and cleaned out of his system all that blighting Bog-**BILE** he can get thankfully back to the more serious and urgent business of writing his most magnificent *novels*—including a *kick-ass **fitness tract!***—all of which you can readily find at *Amazon.com, Barnes&Noble.com and Borders.com!*

In the meantime he sincerely hopes you will buy his Bog-**BASHING** book so he can go out to eat at a public restaurant at least every once in a while but far more importantly: so he can buy his seven frickin' **RAVENOUS CATS** a higher and better grade of frickin' **CAT FOOD!!!**

Tell your friends: this is the **ULTIMATE** sanity-survival manual to visiting and living in the sanity-threatening Bog written *honestly*(at last!)and especially for students studying at Cal, graduating from high school or transferring from college or university to attend Cal(or foolishly considering it though they should wisely **RE**-consider it!)as well as for all current natives and residents already squatting in the Bog along with all those even remotely *thinking about* visiting or moving to the Bog(though they should wisely think better *of* it!)! This guide will effectively help them *seriously* think it *over* and *through* enough(hopefully)to make them change their minds!

www.ingramcontent.com/pod-product-compliance
Lightning Source LLC
Chambersburg PA
CBHW021227090426
42740CB00006B/412